HB 12.1

Run With Endurance the Race God Set Before You

Julie Wages

HB 12.1: Run With Endurance the Race God Set Before You
Copyright © 2019 by Julie Wages

ISBN 978-0-359-63099-8

Acknowledgements

Hilary Charlet my editor – Thank you does not say nearly enough how grateful I am for your assistance with this book! You are an extremely talented writer, and I am truly blessed that you partnered with me on this!

www.sweetteabythetree.com

sweetteabythetree@gmail.com

Scott Hennenfent cover design – Thank you so much for making my vision a reality! It turned out so much better than I could have imagined!

www.hennenfentgraphicsdesign.com

scotthennenfent@hotmail.com

David McKeown – Words cannot describe how grateful I am for your assistance in these final stages of this process. I absolutely couldn't have done it without your ideas, input, and encouragement! THANKS LIL BRO!

To my family and friends – There are too many of you to list you individually. I am grateful to each and every one of you and your encouragement through my life, my running journey, and this book!

To my readers – Thank you! Ironically, I am not a "reader", so one of the goals of this book was that you find it easy to read. My intention was that you feel as though I am sitting with you and telling you my story face-to-face. In that, please offer grace to any grammatical, typos, etc. errors that you find. We have edited a LOT, but I'm sure there are things we missed. Thank you for reading, and I truly hope you enjoy my story!

Foreword

Run with endurance!

No one other than Julie could have written this book. It is so personal and yet inspiring. Once you start you won't be able to put it down!

I actually started reading when I brought the book up on my I-pad and began my usual, daily walk on my treadmill, (now called the dreadmill after reading the book). It drew me in so much that before I knew it, I had walked five miles instead of my normal four miles!

Julie's easy-to-read style and her study put into print on how she honed her running style, gives interesting facts that would help the first-time or the long-time runner! Added to all this is Julie's personal story which is laced with how God has led and influenced her life! I may have been the initial inspiration to her taking up running, but she has taken it further than I could have ever imagined.

She makes the thought of taking up running an exciting adventure; the motivation to keep running through pain, rewarding; and the challenge to finish the race well with endurance, inspiring. I recommend this writer and book without hesitation.

Whatever sphere of life you feel challenged to - get up and run for the finish line. Julie Wages will show you that you can do it!

Run with endurance Julie, you're inspiring those running behind you to do the same! Thank you for an incredible read!

John King
Senior Pastor
Riverside Community Church
Peoria, IL

Introduction

God's Awesome Puzzle Pieces of My Life!

Have you ever just looked back on your life and noticed God's puzzle pieces? Have you noticed pieces that seemed insignificant or seemed to make no sense were actually pivotal in the way a situation worked out? Can you also look at those pieces and realize that God was the one that orchestrated all of that for you? This book is full of some of these pieces/moments/encounters that I have experienced. Even as I'm writing it, I sit here and say "Wow! Really God? That's why you did that? Thank you!" Some of these have been obvious as they were happening or shortly after that. Others have taken me YEARS to see.

As I have shared some of these stories over the years, my friends and family have often said, "You should write a book." My response was always, "Oh, yeah, I don't think so." Clearly, since you are reading this, something in that changed. As people kept telling me that more and more often, the seed started to take root, not fully, but a little. I was writing and sharing more of my stories and people did seem pretty interested in them, and more importantly they seemed to be positively impacted by them.

The movie *I Can Only Imagine* came out on March 16, 2018. (If you know me, you are probably saying, "What in the world does that movie have to do with her story?") I saw the movie on March 17 with some women from our Bible Study. It instantly became one of my favorite movies EVER, but for a much different reason that you probably think. I realize the main story is one of redemption, and that in itself was AMAZING. However, for me the movie took on a totally different purpose.

The movie is the story of his life and his journey. How he learned, grew, changed, dreamt, struggled, and listened to God. It was told in such a relatable way that no matter what your life story is, you can understand his story. I realized that I have a story too, not nearly as dramatic and impactful as his, but it is still a story. And, I realized that this is a story that God wants me to share with people outside my close circle of family and friends. As I watched that movie, I knew without a doubt that God was telling me, "It is time, I want you to write a book." It was an absolutely unmistakable nudge.

In case I wasn't quite sure or wasn't quite getting the nudge, He gave me another clear nudge a couple days later. A friend had given me a daily devotional book, and the passage on March 19 was the "hit me over the head with a hammer" moment. It was a story about a very successful doctor that had fallen sick. He was bedridden for quite a long time and was frustrated because he was no longer able to help the sick. He decided to start writing. He decided to write a little bit every day, and he set a goal of 500 words per day. He was successful in that and is now an extremely successful author. As an author he was able to positively impact and help many more people than he could have as a doctor.

I knew this was again God saying to me, "This is what I want you to do, and here is how I want you to do it." So, I started. My goal was 500 words per day. That may sound like a lot to you, but in reality, 500 words on most days was a super easy goal to reach. I did struggle from time to time and didn't make my daily goal. In fact, there were times I would go a week or 2 without writing at all. Not because I didn't have anything to write, but because I let life get in the way and let the enemy's distractions keep me from doing it.

Often times though, when I would get back at it, I would then do about a week's worth at a time. It was scary. Writing a book was quite intimidating. However, I knew without a doubt God wanted me doing it. These were just lies from the enemy trying to keep me from doing it, and I just needed to keep pushing forward.

It's pretty funny actually because this is very similar to how my running journey has played out. I just had to try and keep moving forward. I kept saying, "I'm not a writer". And then it hit me one day, "Well you didn't used to be a runner either and look at you now."

I'm grateful for the path that has gotten me here and super excited about what God still has in store. I hope this book brings you joy, hope, encouragement, and recognition of God's love for you! He loves each of us, and He has a plan and purpose for each of us. Maybe your thing isn't running or writing, but if you listen, I promise you God will tell you what He wants you doing! He will reach you in ways He knows He can reach you. We all have different triggers so the way I "hear" Him is probably completely different than how you "hear" Him. And you know what? That's totally ok. That's how He wants it! We just need to be ready and willing to hear Him.

For more on my running journey and where God is leading me next, you can find me on social media at

Instagram - juliehb12.1
Facebook - Julie Wages

So, here is my story.

Chapter One

Some background (hang with me through this - I promise there is a reason you need this info)

We moved into our home in December of 1998. We live in a small town in Illinois. By small, I mean around 1400 people. At that time, it was my husband Greg, our daughter Ashley, and myself. Mckenzie was born in July 2000. This is when we became the family of 4 that we are today. As I write this, Ashley is now 25 and living on her own, and Mckenzie (Kenzie) is now 18 and just went away to college.

At the time, Greg was coaching the freshman boys' basketball team at a nearby High School. He had been driving back and forth from Peoria (roughly a 45-minute drive each way) for practices and games, and it just wasn't a good fit. It seemed logical that we try and move closer for him. However, shortly after we moved, he moved up to the Fresh/Soph level at a different school. He was now back to a commute, but his dedication and love for coaching made it worth it to him in the end. He continued there for the next 3 seasons.

Whether you have ever moved to a new location or stayed put and had someone new move in next to you, the thought of new neighbors can be pretty stressful. We didn't have to worry about that because we were blessed with some incredible neighbors. The family on the south side of us have been fantastic! The blessings from having them next door are too numerous to even count! It was impossible back then to know the significance of God placing us in this town right next door to this family. But, looking back on it, this was a vital piece to His puzzle.

Rob, the husband/father, was a runner - a very serious runner. The entire family, in fact, had been involved in running and races for many years. He would often tell us about a 10-mile training run he had just completed that seemed to him as though it was really nothing. Over the years with his work schedule and other responsibilities, his running has slowed down. He still runs when he can, just not like he did back then.

I remember thinking, "You ran 10 miles? How in the world do you do that? There is no way I could ever run 10 miles! I can't even run a block!" I literally laugh out loud thinking about the irony of this at this point. Back then running 10 miles seemed more than impossible for me. These were God's seeds being planted. They would take years to grow, but again were vital to this journey.

Debbie, the wife/mother, rescued me MANY times when Kenzie was a baby. Kenzie would only nap for about 30 minutes at a time. This obviously made it difficult to try and complete tasks around the house like laundry, dishes, cleaning, etc. They loved taking her, and they LOVE babies, so this was a perfect fit for all of us. She also spent many afternoons/evenings sitting with us outside as the girls played in her backyard. She would just chat with me, and we would watch them play. She was trying way back then to bring up God and church and in her own non-pushy way try to encourage me to pursue Him.

I have always had a relationship with God, but not always with the church. I grew up going to a Methodist church with my parents. There was absolutely nothing wrong with this or the church. But, it was obvious I needed something different than that as an adult. I just don't remember "getting it" back then. We went because our parents made us and really had no idea what was being taught.

Looking back, this is really where Debbie came into play in trying to bring me to a new relationship with God. I'm so appreciative of that! More seeds being planted. Again, they would take years to grow, but they were planted, and that is the first step. God is so good at that!

Let's fast forward a couple years to when Kenzie was almost 3. I had been working retail in Peoria, which was again about a 40-minute commute each way. I realize this isn't much for some, but it just wasn't what I wanted to do, and it didn't work for my family very well. I wanted to work closer to home and have more flexibility in my work hours so that I could be home for the girls when they needed me.

In talking to Debbie, she had friends that were the owners of a local business. They were looking for someone to come in and work part-time as a receptionist. I did a lot of office work at home helping Greg with his insurance business, so I certainly had the background, and Debbie thought this would be a perfect for me. She mentioned me to them, and that's how the new chapter of my work life started.

This, if I'm honest, was nothing I would've ever dreamt I would be doing. However, it was close to home and just seemed like the right thing to pursue. Clearly, it was the right decision and perfect piece in God's puzzle because 15 years later I'm still there! They are wonderful to work for and have been so flexible over the years in helping with whatever came up. Our clients have been a real blessing to me as well. They are so special! I know them, they know me, we're more like a family than just another office, or at least that's how I feel.

Shortly after I started working there one of the families from the office was heading to Disney World. We had already been a couple times, and this was their first time. They have a daughter the same age as Ashley, and their other daughter is a year younger than Kenzie. I gave them a few pointers to help them on their adventure.

They all had a great time, especially the youngest daughter. She wouldn't stop talking to me after the trip compared to being super shy and not wanting to say a word before they went to Disney. In her defense, however she was probably only 2 or 3 at the time. Disney was our magical connection.

Fast forward some more. Ashley was now in 6th grade, and it was getting close to basketball season. She had grown up on the bench of her dad's High School boys' teams watching him coach. She fell in love with the game as much as he did. I don't remember the specifics, but they weren't going to have a coach for her girls' team. Ashley and most of her fellow 6th-grade girls all decided to take it upon themselves to find a coach. They all signed their names on a napkin at lunch one day with a note asking Greg personally to coach their team. How could he turn that down? They desperately wanted to play and couldn't do it without a coach. The way it all happened was just so special.

Now, back to the family at work that went to Disney. Remember they have a daughter Ashley's age? She too wanted to play basketball. The other dad heard that Greg was going to possibly coach, and he also happened to be a fan and player of basketball, so he told me to let Greg know that if he wanted any help coaching that he would be willing to step in and help.

These are the Joneses - Jeff, Jody, Olivia, and Lauren. Olivia is the daughter Ashley's age and Lauren is the one that wouldn't talk to me until after she went to Disney. Through this basketball adventure, our families became VERY close. We did just about everything together - dinner, movies, pulling loose teeth, and even Thanksgiving dinners.

They went on another Disney adventure a couple years later. This time we were able to let Lauren borrow some of Kenzie's Disney outfits. We had her all set up with princess and other character outfits - another pivotal bonding moment for all of us.

They had been attending a church in Peoria, Riverside Community Church. It is appropriately named as it sits a few blocks off the riverfront in Downtown Peoria. Funny side note - this is the exact same church Debbie and her family were all going to at the time. Again, God is so great with all these details.

They had a great youth program for high schoolers in which Olivia was getting very involved. She invited Ashley and some of the basketball girls to start going with her whenever they had special events. Ashley was enjoying this so much that it led to her and Kenzie beginning to attend church with them on Sundays. This only lasted a few times before I started thinking, "If my girls are going to go to church, I should be the one taking them, not some other family." I decided I would give it a try. So, on Valentine's Day weekend in 2010, my girls and I made plans to go to church together along with the Joneses. Clearly, they were excited. I was finally willing to go, and they wanted to be there by my side for encouragement.

Unlike any other church I had attended over the years, Riverside Community Church commonly showed video clips during the message from either movies or shows that demonstrated part of the message they were trying to deliver. I thought this was a great tool in that it gave a visual that was very relatable to the Pastor's message.

The message that day was on jealousy. Jealousy on Valentine's weekend? That seemed quite an appropriate topic, right? And the video clip? This is where it gets really good!... was from Beauty and the Beast.

We had been to Disney World as a family about 7 times at this point, and each time I was becoming more and more of a fan. So, this video clip was absolutely no accident! This was God speaking directly to me letting me know this church was EXACTLY where He wanted me to be!

Sometimes the hints, nudges, etc. are subtle, but I think in this case He knew I needed something much more obvious. Well, it doesn't really get much more obvious than that. From then on, the girls and I continued attending Riverside with the Joneses.

Each Sunday we went to church it felt as though the message was being spoken directly to me. Any issues I was struggling with were made into the message. I realize that the messages were touching everyone else too in some way. That's how God works. However, I hadn't experienced anything like this before. I was learning about God and my relationship with Him was really starting to grow.

Chapter Two

New Years' Service 2010

I am originally from Missouri, and most of my family still lives there. Kenzie and I had gone out of town to visit some of this family for New Years. We, therefore, were out of town for the holiday and the New Years' service. The Joneses, however, were at the service. Our Pastor had a message involving plans for the new year. He had a resolution/challenge of sorts for the congregation. Clearly, since it was New Years that seemed appropriate as many people are generally trying to make resolutions for the new year anyway.

He wanted to get at least 100 people from our church to participate in the 4-mile Steamboat Classic Race in June. There are 3 races to choose from in this event, but he wanted us to do the 4-mile race. This race starts and ends in downtown Peoria.

His goal was to encourage us to get in spiritual shape as well as physical shape. Having this goal in front of us gave us something to work towards. He chose this particular race because the course actually runs in front of our church. He also wanted to get a group of churchgoers to be on the church steps out front the morning of the race to cheer on the runners. This would let people know our church was there and that they were welcome to join us anytime.

I was speaking with Jody and asked her what Pastor King wanted us to do for the new year. She proceeded to tell me about this running thing. I remember my reaction was something like "Running? Really? I don't run!! How in the world?" I did some exercise videos on a semi-regular basis but never did any cardio or running. I hated cardio! As far as running went, any time I ever tried I wound up stopping because I would always wind up with a pain in my side. I assumed running just wasn't my thing.

It is probably safe to say that becoming a runner would've been in about the top 10 list of things I wasn't planning on ever doing. I didn't even go outside much. My neighbors would joke about whether I still lived here or not because they never saw me outside. Ever seen the movie *The Benchwarmers*? If so, I think you can guess where I'm headed with this. My family and friends called me Howie! I would argue that I wasn't quite as bad as Howie. I didn't hide in a closet. But, it helps make my point that this running thing was about as far out there of an idea as you could get.

Since winters in Illinois can be the opposite of ideal for outside running, I had some time before I could see if this was going to work. I kept praying and asking, "God, is this really what you want me to do? Running?" I felt as though He kept telling me, "Yes, it is!" So, I decided I had to at least give it a try.

At this point in my life, one of my part-time jobs was an at-home medical transcriptionist. I remember standing as I was rechecking my transcription files and jogging in place while I edited them. I even put ankle weights on to run in place. It sounds ridiculous now, but somehow it seemed like a good idea at the time. It went ok, but obviously was still a far cry from actually running outside.

Eventually, the weather started getting better, and it was time to take this adventure outside to see what would happen. When I first started running, I literally started running 1 block at a time. I know that too seems ridiculous, but that's precisely what I did. Any other time in my life that I tried to run any sort of distance, as I mentioned before, I would always get a side stitch or stomach cramp. I'm not sure what the "technical term" is, but it was the same pain that hindered me in grade school when running in PE. I remember doing laps around the gym and having horrible pains in my side all the time. As I started 1 block at a time, I was scared of this pain. Since I had no idea what caused the pain at this point, I obviously had no idea when or if it would start, and if it did, how in the world was I going to succeed at long distance running if I got a cramp after a block or 2. Anyway, I got out there and started and was able to go 1 block. The next day I went out and went 1-½ blocks. I can't remember exactly how many days it took, but I was quickly able to run all 4 blocks around my house!

Back then I didn't have a smartphone or any fancy devices to track my running, so I ran and then drove the same route in my car to determine how far I had gone. I quickly figured out that it was ½ mile if I ran all 4 of those blocks. This would prove to be very helpful information as time went on.

I kept adding a block here and there, and before I knew it, I could run an entire mile - 2 laps around the 4-block square around my house - without stopping! This was HUGE! I seriously hadn't run a mile since 8th-grade! I kept running, adding 1 block at a time. At one point I remember hitting the 22 blocks mark. I don't know how many miles that translated into because of course not all our blocks are the same size, but it was over 20 blocks! Wow! Who would've thought?

I zigzagged around blocks so that I could stay close to home and still get in a more significant number of blocks. I thought running down a straight road was too boring and seemed like it took forever without adding a lot of distance. The zigzagging broke up the scenery a little making it feel like I was going further in a shorter area.

My goal for the Steamboat Race was to run ¾ mile and walk the other ¼ mile and continue that throughout the race. This would have had me running 3 miles of the 4-mile race. Coming from the complete non-runner that I was, I was going to be ecstatic with 3 miles. So, in my training, I just kept running a little more and a little more with this goal in mind.

I remember the first time I ran a full 4 miles. It was such an incredible feeling! I remember I texted my brother (he was the star football player in high school and much more the athlete than I ever was) to tell him. His response was, "Was something chasing you?" That was his way of saying he was quite impressed given again that I was not a runner and certainly couldn't be considered an athlete. There went my 3-mile goal. If I could run 4 miles now in a training run, then surely, I could run the entire 4-mile race, right?

It's RACE DAY! June 2011

When the idea was originally brought up, ALL 7 of us (the 4 Joneses, my 2 daughters, and myself) decided we would do this race. Do you want to guess how many of us actually chose to do it? Yep, that's right. Just me. However, they were ALL there at the foot of our church cheering for me as I ran by with their hand-made signs and pompoms. Keep in mind, this race starts at 7:00 am on a Saturday, and we live a solid 45 minutes from the church, so this in itself was a big deal. There they were my very own cheering section.

As an experienced runner now, I can tell you in ANY race seeing familiar faces along the course is a serious game changer. Even seeing random strangers cheering in a race is a huge deal. We struggle in these races, and each of your faces and signs has the potential to give us that extra little push that we so desperately need to just keep moving forward. I cannot emphasize enough the importance of course support. I know this is quite a tangent right here, but if you ever get the opportunity to be a spectator and cheer for a race, please DO. We need you! We count on you to help us get through! And I'm taking the liberty to speak for all runners in this!

Ok, back to the race. The race instructions recommended not using any headphones for safety purposes. Having never participated in a race before, I obeyed. This was tough. I was used to running with my worship music and focusing on the lyrics. At that point, I still didn't have a smart, fancy phone, and the device I used either couldn't shuffle the songs or I didn't know how to make it do so, so my music always played in the same order. I had become quite used to this and began singing the lyrics to myself the best I could to keep me moving forward.

It's funny how you don't realize it, but your body, muscles, and mind can get used to a specific routine. My mind was now programmed, unbeknownst to me, to remember these songs and their lyrics in the order they always played during my training runs. But, as hundreds of runners around me had headphones, I quickly realized this "no headphone rule" was not a "rule" anyone actually adhered to. So, note to self and first race day lesson learned - never do another race without headphones.

This race course covers a residential area in downtown Peoria. It was amazing to see so many of the people that lived on these streets sitting on their front porches, sitting in their yards, and even standing on the street offering high-fives. WOW, it's 7 am on a

21

Saturday, and all these people came out to watch us run. That's fantastic!

There is a point in the course where you have a small down-and-back section. So, in this area you are next to, for a brief time, the people about a half a mile ahead of you. I didn't know this, but there was a group of firefighters that typically run this race in full gear carrying the American flag. I was blessed to get to see them while I ran through this area. That was AMAZING!! Chills and tears!

As we turned another corner, a wonderful resident had a sprinkler set up by the road. If you wanted to get cooled off a bit, it was right there to run through. What a wonderful gesture! Given this race is the middle of June and despite the fact it starts at 7 am, it can still be a very HOT race, so this sprinkler was a welcome highlight.

A little further up the route, the City Water people had a sprinkler of sorts set up in the middle of the street. Again, YAY!! And THANK YOU! A fire truck, music, and firefighters cheering were the next batch of support and fun a little bit further ahead. I could feel that I was getting closer now to the finish as this was probably around the 3-mile mark.

My first goal was obviously to run every step of the 4-mile course. My second goal was to try and do it at a pace of 12 minutes per mile or less.

The last quarter mile (maybe more, maybe less) is all downhill. This is very deceiving!! "It's downhill, oh great, we can go really fast." Not a good choice. It's still quite a distance to the finish line and from what I understand more people injure themselves going downhill than uphill. So, I just kept pushing at my comfortable pace. When you get to the bottom of the hill, you turn a corner and then it's a short, straight stretch to the finish line.

I could see it. I could actually see the finish line, and I was almost to it!! Who would've ever thought?!! WOW! I crossed that finish line having run every single step of that 4 miles and my finish time was just under 48 minutes! Yes, this meant that I achieved my sub 12 min/mile goal!!! In fact, my official pace was 11:58 per mile. I had just completed my first ever 4-mile race!

We hung around the area a little while and happened to see one of the guys from my husband's old softball team (he's a "real" runner). I couldn't hold back my excitement on this achievement, and he was so kind as to congratulate me and even pose for a picture with me to commemorate the miraculous occasion. He is the one that will eventually help me realize that my cramps are due to dairy.

I got to choose where we ate after the race, because eating is a great reward after a good race! IHOP (International House of Pancakes) was the winner, because who doesn't want some yummy pancakes after a big race! After IHOP we headed home for the next best reward after a race...a NAP! I'm pretty sure I slept for 3 hours that afternoon when we got home. I'm sure glad that I currently don't nap for 3 hours after every 4 miles I run! That would NOT be good!

If you have never run a race before or crossed a finish line, I encourage you to do it. Whether you can run, run/walk, or walk crossing the finish line is nothing shy of amazing. All your hard work in training, your mental preparation, and all the thoughts that try and convince you that you can't do it, crossing that finish line makes it all worth it and says, "OH YES I CAN, AND I JUST DID!"

Chapter Three

Indian Creek 5K

My next race came in August 2011 - The Indian Creek 5K. This is a small, local race in the town next to us. It is held the first weekend in August during the Old Settlers Days Weekend festivities. The team that puts on this race does a wonderful job with it. However, this is still the only time I've participated in the race. (You will understand why later.)

For those of you that aren't familiar with race distances and their "names," a 5K is 3.1 miles. By the time you are done with my story you are going to be an expert on race names and distances, just a fair warning right there.

You are probably thinking, "3.1 miles, that's shorter than the 4-miler, this will be a piece of cake." Nope! Every race is so different, whether it's the same distance or not. They each have their own individuality - whether its hills, curves, terrain, landmarks, streets, houses, businesses, or castles (some of my favorites!).

Being a rookie, it was important for me to drive the course before the race. This gave me an idea of what was to come. I needed that visual to help calm my nerves. I drove this course and realized that the first mile was going to be fantastic. It was all flat and then sloped downhill as we headed out of town. However, if you go downhill, at some point, you must come back up, right? Well, yes. The majority of the second mile (at least it felt that way) was then all uphill as you run back to town. I was very thankful to know that ahead of time. Once you reached the top, you were back in town and it was flat the rest of the way. You then basically run a few residential streets and then turn to the next one and back to get your 3rd mile in.

It's RACE DAY!

I don't remember exactly how many runners participated in this race, maybe 100 give or take, so not too big. As I saw from my drive around recon of the race route, the starting line is in the middle of town. They bring out a cannon, yes, a cannon, to start the race. I was not prepared for that. The noise was quite loud and scary, and then there was the smoke. But, it's tradition, and it's unique and it's fun, so I say keep it up. And, unless it's your first time participating, you know to expect it. See, there is always a lesson to be learned in a race.

Off we went. Once I got to the downhill, I remember a lot of people passing me. It didn't bother me though. I remember thinking, "Do you guys realize what happens when you get to the bottom of this hill? I do! A ginormous HILL!" I just let them keep going.

We hit mile 1, and I saw my first familiar face. Brian, who is now part of the leadership team in the new church we go to, was the guy at mile 1 with the stopwatch calling out the times for us. I remember he was yelling times that started with a 9 when I was close enough to hear him. What? Under a 10-minute mile? Seriously? That was a speed record for me at that time. Remember my pace goal just 2 months prior was under a 12-minute mile. I was super excited. However, I knew I would slow down dramatically soon.

Shortly passed the 1-mile mark is the corner that marks the beginning of the hill. Here it came - the never-ending HILL. I was mentally prepared for it. Slow and steady. My goal was to try and maintain a consistent pace while just focusing on continuing to move forward. Remember those people that sped passed me on the downhill? Yeah, now it was my turn to pass them. Probably not all of them, but I passed quite a few. I just stuck to what felt comfortable and normal for me and slowly and steadily just kept moving up the hill. I finally reached the top, YAY!!! But wait, I still had a way to go. Again, this was the first part of August, and the race started at 8:00 am, so it was getting hot fast. I just kept running.

I remember coming to a cross street and seeing an older gentleman standing in his driveway cheering. This was a guy I knew. He brought one of our clients into the office once a month for her appointment. I had no idea he lived there. A big HI and smile and off I went to try and finish this thing.

About that time, I remember a specific song came on my device (because remember - I learned my lesson about running races without headphones). This would be the first of several pivotal songs that have marked my journey. "Tunnel" by Third Day. The line "There's a light at the end of this tunnel" absolutely spoke to me. I was really struggling in the heat and didn't think I could keep going. But, that lyric perfectly placed by God spoke to me and said, "You CAN do this, and you WILL do this, and there will be a great reward when you complete it!" That song at that moment was so important during that race.

To this day, whenever I hear that song, it takes me back to that moment and memory. It also lets me realize how far I've come since then. The most exciting part is that even though there have been MANY lights and MANY tunnels on this running journey, the story is still unfinished. There will continue to be lights and tunnels, as I continue towards "THE" light at the end of "THE" tunnel.

At about this same time, my cheering section consisting of Kenzie, Jody, and Lauren were there at a corner to cheer me on!! That was fantastic! Seeing their faces cheering and knowing they believed in me was precisely what I needed. They were my extra push to keep running towards the finish line. They had confidence in my ability to finish, and I simply needed to grab a hold of that, stay focused, and keep moving forward. I still had a little way to go though, so don't worry, they had plenty of time to walk from where they saw me to the finish line without any risk of missing me finish.

I made it to the finish line, finally. I think my goal time was a 10:00 minute per mile pace. I don't quite remember my time, I think it was around 35 min, so not quite at my 10 min/mile pace, but it was the absolute best I had at that point. I gave it my all! Race number 2 DONE!

Let me tell you that that 5K was WAY harder than the 4-mile Steamboat Race. Steamboat is flat, and the hill in this one just makes it so much more difficult.

This remains the only race that I have ever received a medal for "placing." Thankful for small races!! I got 3rd place in my age group for the women. I'm pretty sure there were only 4 of us in the age group, but hey it's a legit placing medal! Right?!

Jason, if you are reading this, you do a fantastic job with this event! THANK YOU!

Chapter Four

Fall 2011

My daughters and my niece, Nicole, had been part of a dance team for many years. They typically did one big competition each year. This particular dance season, we had decided the competition would be at Walt Disney World in February 2012. Planning for our trip was in full swing, and given my love for planning Disney trips was continuing to grow, I was the one overseeing all the details.

I had by now become, some would say, "obsessed" with Disney, but in a good way of course. They joke that Walt Disney World is my home away from home. I love the memories we have made together there, as we had been 8 times at this point. Much to my family's dismay, I am almost always wearing something Disney. It is sort of my statement, my style. It is a topic of conversation. It's how people can get to know me. I love talking about Disney.

If I happen to not be wearing something Disney, my clients at the office will even comment, "Where's your Disney today?" It's like they have come to appreciate that that is who I am. It's how they have gotten to know me. Through it, I get to tell stories, share dreams, and share memories. I'm pretty sure there isn't a client that comes in the office that doesn't know of my obsession with Disney.

One specific client comes in the office roughly once a month on Fridays right before lunch. She has a daughter that lives in Florida that she goes to visit for an extended period during the winter. (Can you blame her? Winter in Illinois versus winter in Florida? Sign me up!) She and I talk about Disney quite a bit. She typically asks about upcoming trips, past trips, etc.

Now that I've started running, she asks about that too. She was asking about Disney one Friday, and I mentioned that we were headed there in February for my daughter's dance competition. She asked if I had checked to see if any races were going on while we were there. Races? At Disney? There was such a thing? Her daughter had apparently done quite a few Disney races.

At that point, I had no idea Disney had races. I was new to running and wasn't on Facebook or any other social media at that point, so I really had no way of coming across this information yet. Let's be honest, if you aren't a runner and don't hang around runners, you have exactly zero need to know where races are or that they even exist. But, side note, if you do know a runner, even if you aren't one, they will make sure you know when and where the races are whether you think you want to know or not. Just a helpful tip right there.

It turned out that the weekend we were going for the dance competition just happened to be the same weekend as the Princess Half Marathon weekend. Seems ironic, but with God, there is no irony, just a plan!

If you know me at all, when I'm excited about something you know that it's ALL I talk about. So, in this case, pretty much running and Disney. If you want me to talk forever, bring up either of those topics. If you don't want me telling stories, choose just about any other subject, but I will warn you now, I'm pretty sure I can take just about any topic and somehow bring it back to running or Disney and then watch out.

Anyway, because I was so excited about this whole running thing, I talked about it a lot. My sister-in-law, Jennifer, the mom of my niece that was also competing, was a non-runner like I had been 12 months earlier. Seeing how excited I was about it and all the changes in me, Jennifer decided she wanted to give it a try. So, she started working at it a little bit at a time too. Her schedule unfortunately didn't give her as much flexibility in when she could run as mine did, but she was doing her best and making progress.

We decided we needed to do this 5K. I mean after all, we both love Disney, we were going to be there anyway, and it was Princess weekend. No one had to twist our arms for this one.

The race was on Saturday morning, the same day as the dance competition. At that point, they hadn't started offering a 10K (This was great for us because neither of us would've been up for a 10K at that point). The race was super early, so we would have plenty of time to complete the race and get where we needed to be for the competition. There it was, we were signed up for our first Disney race! Let the training begin.

Again, you are probably thinking that clearly, a 5K shouldn't be that tough for me, right? After all, I had now completed two 4-mile races (There was the Hog Days race over Labor Day weekend that was the second 4-miler - I haven't mentioned this race yet) and a really tough 5K. I'm here to tell you, don't take that for granted. Just because you have completed the distance multiple times, doesn't mean that it's going to be easy, especially given I was still in my early stages of training.

I seriously didn't really know what I was doing. I just went out and ran. Again, I didn't have Facebook and Facebook groups to learn from. I did at one point rent a couple books from the library to try and get some insight. I don't remember learning anything monumental, but I'm sure the stories were beneficial at the time.

It's important to remember I live in Illinois. We clearly do not have ideal conditions for outdoor running in the winter. Before all the real northerners start lashing out at me, I know you guys have it much worse. But, relatively speaking, Illinois is not going to prove nice for winter running. As it got colder, I kept trying to run outside. I really tried. I just found that I had trouble breathing. I asked a runner friend, and he said to try and keep my mouth covered. I tried; it didn't help. I just felt like I was gasping for air.

So, I did the only thing I could think of to do, and no, it wasn't "just stop training and wing it." I went to the treadmill. Notice that for now, I'm calling it by its actual name - the treadmill. Currently, I only call it by its runner's nickname - the dreadmill. But, at this stage in the game, I was still a newbie, and 1-3 miles on the treadmill wasn't horrible. So, this was where I spent my time that winter as I was training for this Disney 5K.

I do not have a treadmill at home, but we have an excellent facility here in our small town, it's right next door to where I work. It is a rehab/therapy place, but also has some exercise equipment including multiple treadmills.

Again, I live in a very small town, and everyone is extremely friendly. I met some fantastic people during my time there. They all wanted to hear about what I was training for and thought it was super awesome that I could run so far.

One woman stood out to me. She was so sweet. She could talk to anyone and everyone and always had a smile for you. She and her husband worked out there quite often. I would see them pull up on my days when I was working. They were always there when it opened at 7:00 am. Their dedication was fantastic. I can only hope that I'm that dedicated when I'm their ages.

At some point during this training, I started experiencing some knee pain. I had no idea what was causing it, and it didn't really hurt while I was running so I kept at it. I continued to train on the treadmill and continued planning the Disney trip for the dance team and their families.

At some point, I remember being at Walmart (one of the MANY times I'm there). We were walking through the parking lot to head into the store, and I saw a magnet on a vehicle. It was a pink Mickey shaped magnet with 13.1 on it. Many of you may not even realize what those signify. I sure didn't before I started running. Those are a badge of honor of sorts for us runners. They indicate what type of race we have run. In this case, 13.1 is indicative of a half marathon which is 13.1 miles.

Remember when I promised you would be proficient in the race distances? Here is part of your lesson. If you see 5K that signifies 3.1 miles, 10K = 6.2 miles, 15K = 9.3 miles, 13.1 = half marathon and 13.1 miles, and 26.2 is a marathon and 26.2 miles. I'm not sure why it switches from K to miles, but that's for someone else to figure out. There are higher and more advanced distances as well, but this gives you an idea.

Anyway, when I saw that pink Mickey head magnet, I knew that not only had that driver completed a half marathon but that she had also completed that half marathon at Walt Disney World because of the Mickey head. At that moment I knew that I wanted to earn that magnet. I wanted to earn that pink Mickey head 13.1 magnet. I set this goal for January 2013.

At that point, however, I didn't realize that the pink represented the Princess Half Marathon Weekend. There is a race weekend in

January as well, and that was my goal. Keep in mind I could barely get to 4 miles and had knee pain that I didn't understand, but I figured I had plenty of time to work all that out. We all need to set goals, right? However, as you will soon see, God had a different plan for me than January 2013.

Again, I was the one working with the dance organization on all the logistics for our dance girls and their families for the competition. I was also in charge of planning mine and my in-laws' portion of the trip. Even though they were frequent Disney goer's and loved Walt Disney World, they knew that the planning was my "thing." They let me just take it over and get everything all set up. This is probably near the beginning of when they all started telling me that I should be trying to do that for a living.

February came around, all the planning was completed, and it was now time to travel. We needed dance costumes, race gear, as well as all the Disney "stuff." It's a wonder we fit it all in our suitcases.

It's RACE DAY and Dance Competition Day!!

Saturday morning finally arrived. We got up super early (not all of us) to get ready for the race because it was starting at 5:30 am or some crazy early hour.

There were 11 of us total traveling - my family of 4, my brother David, Jennifer and her family of 4, and my mother and father-in-law. We had a very specific plan for getting everyone where they needed to be that day.

The girls needed to be at the dance competition location by a specific time. We would not be able to get back from the race in time to turn around and get them where they needed to be. So, we left Greg, David, my father-in-law, and my nephew with specific instructions on how to get the girls where they needed to be and when. This included, of course, all their dance gear as well as a small suitcase of my change of clothes and stuff to clean up with after the race. The plan was that we would just meet them at the competition location and clean up and change when we got there. It worked perfectly.

Jennifer and her husband Denny had rented a car, so he drove us to the start of the race. Off we went, Jennifer, Denny, my mother-in-law, and I set out for the race. Having never done a Disney race before, we really had no idea what to expect. In fact, we were new to races in general, so this was a bit overwhelming.

Since the race started so early, it was obviously still pitch-black outside. However, Disney, of course, had everything lit up, music playing, and characters entertaining to keep you lively while waiting for the race to start.

Since this was the Princess Half Marathon weekend, there were a TON of princess type running costumes. I didn't even realize that was a thing. But, yes, costumes for Disney races are DEFINITELY a thing. We even found an older gentleman in a tutu and tiara. We absolutely needed a picture with him. Actually, there were probably lots of them, but this one gentleman stood out to us. That is still one of my favorite pictures.

Clearly, we didn't do costumes, just regular running gear. Again, we were the rookies and I wasn't on Facebook (I'm not in any way trying to push for Facebook, but I will admit that over the years it has been a fantastic tool for me to learn more about this stuff) yet to have learned about all the details of a Disney race.

It was finally time to get to our corral. Back then, you weren't placed in specific corrals for the 5K (this is all different now). We just chose a time that we thought we could maintain and meandered our way into that corral. Our cheering section - Mama and Denny - headed off to wait for us at the finish line.

Keep in mind, my knee had still been bothering me. I had to do this 5K race with a knee sleeve on due to the knee tending to feel like it was going to give out.

Jennifer and I embarked on this journey together. We had no idea what to expect. We quickly learned that there are a lot of people that do these races! There were a lot of people to try and weave in and out of. Trying to stay together was a challenge in itself. We had to zig and zag and run up ahead and slow down so the other could catch up. But, we did it, and we did it together.

Being the huge Disney fans that we are, to have the opportunity to run a race through Epcot was epic! The reality that we were actually running through the World Showcase was just amazing! And then we saw Spaceship Earth, or as it's more affectionately known by many of us as the Epcot ball, was just a special gift.

Most people don't ever get the opportunity to even visit there. That we not only got to visit but now to take that to another level and run there was the start of just some fantastic and unbelievable adventures. Obviously though, at that point, I had no idea the opportunities and plan God had in mind, but for now, this was a fantastic gift He had given us.

We finished that race together. We didn't have any super speedy times or anything like that, but we did it. We had completed our first 5K at Walt Disney World. We found our cheer squad, eventually. It's hard to track people down in a sea of thousands of people, but we did. One of the lessons all 4 of us got from this was, wear something that stands out. Your cheer squad is trying to scan through literally thousands of other runners to find you, and as the runner, you are trying to find your cheer squad amid literally who knows how many more thousands of people.

How we actually found each other was really a miracle in itself. Looking back now on what I know about these races, I cannot believe that they actually found us. Thank you, Jesus! Off we went to join the rest of the family at the dance competition with our first Disney medals proudly around our necks!

We made it in plenty of time for the girls' performances. They all did fantastic jobs. Hopefully, they understand how big the opportunity to participate in a dance competition at Disney World is as well. Again, not everyone gets to see Disney World, but to be able to visit and compete in something you love at the same time is such a gift! We were all having wow moments on that trip!

God was definitely planting a lot of seeds and forming a lot of essential puzzle pieces in this season. I had no idea at the time that that was happening. As I write this and am remembering how this all transpired and how the future after this played out, I'm again sitting here just like WOW God, you really are amazing!

Chapter Five

Summary 2012

As my distances started increasing in the second year, I needed to start running in some straighter lines despite not really wanting to do that. It simply was the most logical way to increase the distance. I got further away from home and could cover larger amounts of town this way.

As I did this, my knee pain and instability started getting better. I didn't realize that the continuous turning at corners was causing issues with my leg and in turn, causing my knee to feel somewhat unstable. This is definitely not a good thing when you are a runner. So, another lesson learned, and my confidence grew because I didn't have to constantly worry about my knee and how to fix it.

It's RACE DAY!!!! - Steamboat Classic 2012

Here it is again, the race that started it all. Our church had designed shirts for those that wanted them so that we would all match for the race and be recognizable.

This would be the first time in this process that a specific Bible verse became important to me. The journey had been guided more with song lyrics and attending church on a regular basis rather than specific Bible verses. On the front of our shirts was the church logo. On the back was "I will finish the race. Hebrews 12:1". I'm not sure there is a Bible translation that has that specific wording or if it's probably more of a paraphrase but, that was perfect for me. This was simple and easy for me to understand and remember. I was going to finish that race! Little did I know how much more that verse meant for this journey.

By putting that on the backs of our shirts, the hope was that it would inspire someone behind us to keep pushing forward in the race as well as remind them about Jesus. That's a pretty big thing in races, reading the shirts of the people in front of you. I know I touched on it before, but this goes along with the signs from the spectators. You have no idea how beneficial those are to us. I'm here to tell you that we are so appreciative of that! They can literally change a race for us. It's that one verse, that one phrase, that one word, that one joke, that one picture that can keep us moving forward and give us the needed push to keep going.

This time, a couple of my friends joined me for the race. We didn't run together but having them run the race was just priceless to me! It started with just me, and now we were up to 3. Who knew? I set a new PR for myself at this race. I cut 6 minutes off my time from the previous year! I was ecstatic!

The knee, unfortunately, was still a battle as I continued to keep running. Although it seemed somewhat better, it still would have some unstable feeling moments. I was still fairly sure it wasn't anything significant or an actual injury, it was just a battle I was having to overcome. I was trying to run four days a week with back to back days on Wednesday/Thursday. I think I was consistently running about 20-22 miles a week. Which, I didn't realize back then, was quite a bit. However, I was only able to get to a total of about 6 miles for my longest run.

I noticed an ad in our local paper about a group of runners that were starting a team for the Kewanee to Peoria St. Jude Satellite Run. They were looking for runners that wanted to join them. I didn't notice this until about six weeks before the event. I knew, due to my knee, I couldn't participate, and given it was a fundraiser, I didn't have enough time to raise the money. However, it ignited a new fire within me, and I became determined to get better so I could do it the following year.

To be honest, I didn't even really know what it was or that it existed before seeing the ad. I remember on one of my runs a local guy that often passed me in his truck while I was on a training run stopped and hollered from his truck, "Did you make a wrong turn? Shouldn't you be in Memphis?" That must've been early August my first year. I laughed and agreed, but really, I didn't know what he was talking about. Since I wasn't a runner previously, this wasn't something I paid any attention to.

The St. Jude Run is a huge event. Over 30 teams start from their respective towns and run relay-style all the way into downtown Peoria, IL. The primary team is the Memphis to Peoria team. That's how it all started. They drive to Memphis and tour the St. Jude Hospital and then begin their journey back here. This is a 4-day journey back for them. Most of the satellite teams are from Illinois, but there is a St. Louis team and at least one other Missouri team. There is also at least one team from Iowa.

The Kewanee route is a 54.5-mile journey and is the only team that comes through our small town. They stop at our town square for a few minutes for a little break, and runners hoped to have people come to cheer them on as they came through. I insisted that

Kenzie and I go up to cheer them on. If I couldn't run with them, I wanted to at least be there as they came through town. I just had that feeling it was something we HAD to do. You know that feeling? You can't dismiss it, you may not know why, but you know you have to do something. Well, I'm here to tell you that is God telling you that is what He wants you to do.

There were less than 20 of them that first year and it was terribly hot. Thankfully, that group was made up of super strong runners and they were able to run despite all of that. Still, that was not an ideal-sized group for that lengthy of a journey in that heat. It was awesome to see them come in. So inspiring! They seemed so excited and just so genuinely happy to have the opportunity to do this. I committed to God, to myself, and to Kenzie that I would be on that team no matter what the next year.

It's RACE DAY - Steamboat 2013

This was a special race. Jennifer had gotten quite a few of our friends and family to commit to doing this race. It fell on her 40th birthday, and it was the 40th anniversary of the race itself. This was the first and only race that all my family (Greg, Ashley, Kenzie, and myself) participated in. We didn't plan to run together as we were all different speeds, but just having them running the same race was super awesome to me! I usually am excited on race day, even though we get up at some crazy early time, but this time I was ecstatic! It was the excitement like we were leaving for Walt Disney World!

Ashley and Kenzie had trained a few times together, so we planned that they would run together. It still made me nervous just letting Kenzie loose in the race without having someone near her to keep an eye on her. She was almost 13 and I know I'm protective, but the buddy system never hurt anyone right?! I realized that she was safe as there were hundreds of other runners around her and the level of actual danger in that environment was low, but you never know. And, this was her first race. So, yes, overprotective mom kicked in.

Anyway, the plan was that the girls would stick together. They were going to start around the 11 minutes per mile pace. I chose to start in the 9-minute pace area. I had no intention of being able to maintain a 9-minute mile, but my first mile was always the slowest. I was hoping for a decent time for this one, something under 40 minutes, so I wanted to try and get a good start. I figured if I started with the faster people that maybe it would help me get set at a good pace from the beginning. Obviously, with the race only being 4 miles, if you had a slow first mile, you don't have a lot of mileage to make up a ton of time. This also ensured that Greg and I would finish before Kenzie so that one of us at least could find her as soon as she finished if she and Ashley got separated. He and I weren't running together, but I knew we would both be fast enough to finish well before her.

I was about half a mile maybe a little more into the race, and someone was tapping on my arm. It was Kenzie. Wait, what? "What are you doing up here?" She had lost Ashley in the crowd of people, because she was better at zigging and zagging through them, and then she just apparently started running at an almost sprinting pace. I told her she was now going to stay with me.

She hadn't trained anywhere close to the speed we were currently traveling at, and I knew she wouldn't be able to pace herself at this point for the rest of the 4 miles. So, I kept her with me and slowed her down a little. If I'm good at anything in this running stuff, I'm good at keeping a steady pace despite whatever everyone else is doing around me. I can keep a solid pace that I know will allow me to finish whatever the race is I'm currently running. I think that was learned through training by myself all the time.

So, there we were running together for almost the entire race. I had set my phone to let me know every quarter mile what our pace was. I still knew we were going too fast and was continuously checking with her to see if she was ok. I'm pretty sure she was quite over my "momming" by the time we got done. But, I had to be sure. She hadn't fueled or hydrated very well. She had soda and nachos for lunch the day before. I was like, "Um this is not good race food." But, she was young, and they can handle a lot more than I can, and again there are always lessons to be learned. She made it through the race. We made it to the finish line together. Afterward, her official time was a tiny bit ahead of mine because she had started behind me. So, she, of course, had to brag that she beat me. I, of course, then had to make sure everyone knew that she was only able to do it because I paced her through the whole thing.

It was a great race, and I cherish being able to do that with her right by my side. As a runner, when you run with people that are close to you, it just makes it even more of a wonderful experience! However, it was our first experience with me playing the "trainer/coach" role, and needless to say, I didn't play that role very well. The mom in me was way more evident as I constantly was asking, "Are you ok? Do we need to stop? There's water coming up do you want some?" There are worse things I could've been saying right?!

Chapter Six

St. Jude Run 2013

I stuck to my commitment that I would join the Kewanee to Peoria St. Jude Run Team. I had a dedicated training plan and was pushing myself to train hard. I had initially set my goal at 10 miles. However, I was able to manage a 10-mile training run that summer, so I had to set my goal a little higher. I pushed it to 10-15 miles.

The whole thing was so new to me. I had no idea what to expect. I didn't know anyone on my team as there was no one from my town doing the run. There were a couple of people from a neighboring town, but I didn't know them personally. If you know me at all, you know that this is absolutely not something I would generally agree to do. I like to feel comfortable and familiar with my environment. I don't reach out and strike up conversations with strangers. Once I know you, I will talk forever, but that takes quite a while. This was different though. I was certain God wanted me to do this run, and I was willing to say yes to it. Knowing that God wanted me to do it gave me the confidence and courage to commit and follow through. This too will become a common theme for me.

Don't get me wrong. It doesn't mean that fear doesn't still creep in, because it absolutely does. But, fear is a lie from the devil, and we need to push that aside and focus on God. I promise you this, if it is something God wants you to do, He will give you the courage, tools, and strength to follow through.

I honestly cannot remember if the 10-miler was my longest run or if I had gone further, and since I can't remember, I know that it's not essential. The details I'm able to share in all this are so specific and clear in my memory that I know that's God telling me, "This is what I want you to share."

It's RUN DAY! It isn't a race, so we can't really say "it's race day."

The day of the run finally came. We had made a detailed plan. My family was in Monmouth for a huge car show. This had become a tradition for them. They spent the night there, so I had been left to mentally prepare myself for whatever was in store. I was going to drive myself to Kewanee and leave my car. Greg and one of his buddies were going to drive home with the show cars and then head back to Kewanee to get my car. It's crazy to think this was so long ago that Kenzie wasn't even close to being old enough to have her license yet. Anyway, they were going to do all of that and be back to Wyoming by the time we were arriving sometime between 9 and 10.

The start of our run is so special. We have a few St. Jude patients affiliated with our team, and they are our official starters. We take a few group photos, and with their mark, we begin our journey. We are escorted through Kewanee with fire trucks. I'm pretty sure the locals aren't too happy when they have sirens and horns blaring at 5:15 am, but no one has complained enough that we have to stop doing it. I assume they realize why we are doing it and therefore are totally supportive.

There aren't too many people out at that hour to cheer us on, which is understandable. As we reach the main road and pass McDonald's and the gas station, we start to get some fans. They are mostly family and friends of runners, but it is still wonderful to see them out there supporting us.

We have a list detailing our route and the lengths of each leg. This marks where we start and stop and take breaks, etc. I had planned in my head which legs I wanted to try and run, based on their length, the location, the time of day, etc. The team wants everyone to run the first leg and the last leg and whatever they want in between. There is no pressure ever to run if you don't feel that you can. We are blessed with a long enough route that whatever distance goal you may set for yourself you really can try and obtain it. We also are blessed with enough runners now that there is never a shortage of runners that are willing to be out there. The only issue is the "fast legs." There aren't that many people that are capable of the speed, so those generally consist of only about three runners.

I wanted to run into both Toulon and Wyoming. There is an intersection that marks one of our stops that then heads us into Toulon. I planned to rest after the initial leg until that intersection and then start running. I'm usually better at just running first thing in the morning and not stopping until I'm done, but the two legs leading up to this were way too hilly and too long that I knew they weren't for me. I also wanted to be able to experience running into the towns as I knew that's where the people and, more importantly, my people were going to be.

This stretch from the intersection into Toulon was about a 3.1-mile stretch, yep a 5K for those keeping track. It was two different legs so that anyone that wants to join the last bit and run into Toulon didn't have to run the whole 3-mile stretch at one time. I chose to run both legs.

While on that stretch, cars would occasionally have the opportunity to pass us. As they went by, they generally would honk and wave and cheer. It was so awesome! Jennifer and Nicole (my niece) were one of those cars. They came up beside us cheering and honking very loudly. Nicole had made a poster for me and was holding it out the window. That visual is forever in my heart and mind. They were headed into Toulon to cheer us on as we came into town. They were my first familiar faces of the day, and what a special moment that was. It gave me an extra burst of energy and joy. I was doing this! I was really doing this!

I knew that there was supposed to be a group of my friends waiting for us when we got to Toulon, and I could not wait to see them. I had positioned myself towards the back of the pack as I knew I wasn't a strong runner. We were supposed to go at a pace everyone could handle. I felt comfortable in my zone, and the women around me agreed it was a good pace, and we hoped the ones in front would maintain what we were doing. This group of us back there started chatting and sharing. I was slow to offer too much, but we had quickly become close. We were kind of like a team within a team. There was one woman that was a really strong runner. She was gracious enough to stay back there with us. Her experience, encouragement, and knowledge were priceless that day. I could not have done what I did if not for her, and I believe quite a few others would say their experience was the same. I am forever grateful.

We made it to Toulon and there they were. My friends and family. There they were, their precious, familiar faces. I was so happy to see them!

We stopped in Toulon for breakfast, but I couldn't eat. My stomach doesn't allow me to eat much while running, and I knew better than to try. So, I just chatted with them while everyone else rested and had breakfast.

One of the unique things about this run is that there is a local 5K that happens on the same morning in Toulon. It's the Indian Creek 5K. Yes, that's the run I had done in my first year with that huge hill. In fact, because of this run, it is essential that we arrive in Toulon by 7:45 so that they can easily start their race at 8:00 without us having to block both sides of the road. It's also nice because they are there to support us as we come into town, and then we get to return the favor as they start their race. We line the streets and cheer them on as they begin their journey.

We then headed to Wyoming. My mother and father in-law live right off the road we were running on. She had made a sign and put it in her window, so I could see it as we went by. I didn't run that leg because it's a 4-mile leg. I did, however, make sure that I saw the sign as we rode by in the RV.

I didn't think I could do that leg followed by the 2-mile leg that went into Wyoming. I HAD to run into Wyoming since that's where I live. I just wasn't strong enough at that point, especially given I had already run almost 5 miles. But, it was my goal to do that by the next year.

We made it into Wyoming, and how wonderful that was! My family and friends were all gathered together to see our team and me. Some were the same from Toulon, but others had joined them now in Wyoming. I'm not sure they will ever know how much it means when I see their faces in these events. It is priceless! I gave them a quick recap of how the morning had been going so far, gave them hugs, and it was time to get back on the road.

My next planned leg was one leg later. So, I had a leg to rest a bit. I wanted to run here because a couple I know were going to be out there cheering for us and giving us water bottles. They are the grandparents of a local St. Jude patient. She is my daughter Ashley's age and has been fighting an unimaginably tough battle since shortly after high school. I was running for her and all the other kids just like her. I needed to run this leg for her and to be able to see her grandparents as they supported us.

This was a tough, tough leg. Not just because of the emotional side, but because it was getting warmer, I was going to be over 10 miles after this leg, and we hadn't even made it to lunch yet. Also, keep in mind, I hadn't eaten anything since I left home due to my stomach issues. The path was a bunch of rolling hills. They weren't big, but at that point, they sure seemed like it. None of that mattered though. I just keep trying to run. It wasn't a pretty leg for me by any means, but I did it. Now, I could rest for a while. We were almost at our lunch stop.

I knew that once I had some lunch, I wouldn't be able to run for a while, and that was ok. There were a lot of hills coming up, and well, you are probably starting to get the picture that hills are not my friend. At this point, my stomach was in full-on "I hate you" mode. It just would not calm down. Anything I ate or drank just set it into turmoil. I just tried not to eat or drink anything, and while I was running, it seemed ok. So, that became my strategy for as long as it would take me.

I managed a few more legs as the afternoon went on. I had seriously never done anything this hard in my life. Again, that was ok. We were doing this for kids that fight cancer. I don't care how hard running seems; it doesn't come close to what they battle every day.

I remember on one of the legs that I happened to be running the Joneses passed us on their way home from Peoria. They knew the route and purposely took that road hoping to see us. Even though they were just passing on the other side of the road, the honks and waves were again so vital. I will never forget the feeling of seeing them there, again priceless!

We then turn onto Knoxville Ave. This is a busy main road that goes through Peoria. There were some shorter legs on this part of the route, so I chose to run again. This was amazing. There were so many cars and so many people.

There is a trailer court area that we go past, and a wonderful woman came running from there to give us a donation. There are a lot of businesses as well. One of which is a car dealership. There was a group of salesmen that came out to cheer us on as we passed. Traffic was stopped at an intersection, all except us, to give us a safe path through. Cars that passed right next to us would honk and wave. Kids in the back seat were yelling for us. It was so amazing!

Knowing that ALL these people knew what we were doing and why we were doing it was so awesome. Words cannot describe it. This was so much more than just us or even the 30+ other teams. It was also an entire city that had all joined together to support the children and families of St. Jude! To be a small part of that is just such a wonderful blessing.

I finished that day with a little over 16 miles! And more importantly, thanks to my wonderful and generous family, friends, and community I raised over $1,200 for St. Jude that year! What a fantastic event and I'm so thankful to be a part of it.

Chapter Seven

Hog Days, Labor Day weekend 2013

Remember when I mentioned there was a second 4-mile race that I had run? You were probably thinking, "What? She didn't tell us about that one. Where did that one come from?" Well, here you go.

The two years prior to this I had run this race. However, not every race I run has a super significant "God moment." It certainly doesn't mean that those races weren't special and hadn't been pivotal parts of my journey, because their meaning is quite contrary. I just don't feel that there is a message in them that God wants me to share with you. I mean, let's be honest, if I recapped every single race, it would take you forever to get through this book. So, my goal here is to make sure I give you what God wants me to give to you.

The Hog Days Stampede (yep that's its actual name!) is a small, local race in a town near us called Kewanee (yes, the same town that the St. Jude Run starts in). It is a 4-mile race held on the

Saturday of Labor Day weekend. It's in the middle of the weekend-long celebration called Hog Days.

As I mentioned, I had run this race the two years before this, but this time I had some company. Bobbie, my youngest sister, and her family came up for the weekend to camp with us, and she had agreed to run it with us. Her husband, Jeremy, also decided to run again; he had run the previous year. Our friend, Roger, who always seems up for a race, also planned to run. And, finally, Kenzie had decided to give another go at this running a race thing.

I was still pretty sore from the St. Jude Run (I'll get more into that in a little bit), but I still wanted to run. I was more than happy to run with Bobbie and/or Kenzie if they wanted me to. Bobbie, unfortunately, couldn't train as much as she would've liked, but she had always been extremely active and athletic, so we were confident she would be fine for the race.

The 3 of us started together, but Kenzie quickly just started sprinting. This is her norm even now. I try to encourage her to go slower in the beginning, but like many, she gets so excited about the race and the other runners she starts way too fast. So, Bobbie and I lost track of her early on. We were keeping a pretty good pace ourselves. In fact, we were going much faster than I had anticipated, especially given Bobbie hadn't been able to train for distance. It's one thing to run 1 mile at a certain speed, but to keep that same speed for 4 miles is quite a bit different. As we have already established pacing does seem to be one thing I've gotten good at. If I'm feeling good, I can generally start speeding up the second half of a race.

Given this was Labor Day weekend, it was quite warm. The race starts at 8 am instead of 7 am, so it gets hot quickly which obviously is a factor in how the race goes. The course takes us through a lot of residential areas of Kewanee. It's a fun course as there are usually quite a few spectators outside their homes. However, some small hills sneak up on you.

They don't look like much but when you start going up them in the heat and the fact they are all in the last mile and a half, they can pose quite challenging, especially for people like me that hate hills. And let me clarify, I do know that what I consider "hills" are flat for most of the country. But, for me, they are hills. I hope that one day hills and I become great friends, but for now, they are still, even the small ones, quite the nemesis mentally for me.

Bobbie and I continued. I kept suggesting we needed to slow down a little. She is quite competitive, and I think the people around her kept her wanting to push harder. She was doing a fantastic job. Eventually, though, she needed to take a little walk break and didn't want to do it with me. She was too competitive for that even though I would've had no problem walking with her. She told me to go on ahead and try and find Kenzie.

We were probably into or close to the last mile and a half of the race at this point, and I assumed Kenzie was way too far ahead for me to catch her. A longer race yes, but with only 4 miles, it doesn't leave a lot of room to catch up with someone that you lost in the first couple of blocks.

Bobbie seemed serious, and despite my not wanting to leave her, I did. Occasionally that's the right choice. I kept up a decent pace, and suddenly, I caught a glimpse of Kenzie up ahead. She was walking at this point. I assume she had to take some breaks too, due to going out too fast. I was able to catch up to her because I continued with my steady run. She was so happy to see me. She was struggling and just needed something to boost her confidence a little that she could and would do this. I assured her that we were almost done and encouraged her to keep going.

She was ready to be done, which is often the case for most of us as we get into the last mile or so, regardless the distance of the race. We did a walk/run thing for a bit, and then once we got to the final straight stretch where we could see the finish line ahead, she kicked it up a gear and was able to finish strong.

There is always something about seeing that finish line in front of you that gives you a burst of energy you didn't know you had. It's a great feeling! Bobbie was also able to finish strong. I'm so very proud of both of them!

Races aren't easy mentally, physically, or emotionally. They are very draining. Anyone that starts and finishes a race, no matter the distance or speed, should be extremely proud of that accomplishment. Not everyone can do that or even chooses to try!

Chapter Eight

Fall 2013

Let's go back to the reference I made to still being sore after the St. Jude run. After the run, I could barely walk. I had given every ounce of everything I had that day and was in so much pain that everything was hard. But, it was so worth it! I would do it again in a heartbeat. If running and feeling like that every day could somehow heal all the children at St. Jude, I would do it every single day.

As I was training for the St. Jude run, I had the idea that maybe if it went well, that I should try to do a half marathon. Again, that's 13.1 miles. There was a half marathon in Springfield, Illinois in October. I figured this would be a nice one to try. I had no idea how St. Jude was going to go, so I didn't want to make any definite plans beyond that run. But, if it went well and I could keep up with my distance training, that seemed like the logical next step.

As I tried to get back into a regular running routine, I continued to battle knee pain. I couldn't even run 1.5 miles before it would start hurting. It was a very odd pain in the lower right side of my right knee, but I knew enough not to try to run through it. While doing the St. Jude run it had flared-up horribly and other, more experienced, runners suggested that it could be my IT band (iliotibial band). Of course, at this point, I had no idea what that meant. They suggested stretching it to see if that would help but cautioned me that it could and likely would be a very lengthy process as it is not something that gets un-mad very quickly.

I started doing some research on the internet trying to find some good IT band stretches. I had a series of workout videos that had a stretching video in it. I eventually started doing that video.

I quickly realized that a half marathon in October was not in my cards. There was no way I could be ready by then since I was still trying to get into a regular schedule and trying to get my IT band not so angry with me. That was ok with me as again I knew that if God wanted me to run it, He would've let the knee pain heal and I would be full-fledged into training.

What's fun here and what was a lesson for me (and one that I still continue to learn) is that although I had the idea of running the half marathon in my head, I had to put it in God's hands. Sure, it seemed entirely logical, right? After all, I had completed a 10-mile training run, and I had run 16 miles on the day of the St. Jude run. Surely that meant I was ready for that step.

This entire running journey has been God's plan for me. Even though I have races that I think I want to run, if He doesn't want me to run them, then I just don't run them. I have been able to clearly distinguish between these and follow through with His way.

In other areas of my life, that is a tough pill to swallow so to speak. But, again the lesson I can try and take away from this is that these races are symbolic of everything in my life. I need to give it ALL to Him and let Him guide every single choice. If He doesn't want me to choose a certain way, regardless of how brilliant I think it is and the million reasons I can give as to why it's the best decision, I need to pick His way EVERY SINGLE TIME.

With the help of the stretching video, the IT band became less and less annoyed. It turns out that this had been the issue with my knee the entire time. All those times I kept telling you it felt unstable and was hurting, that was all this.

It's essential to note here that even though I say it was my knee, that isn't fair to the knee. It was the IT band the whole time. The pain just showed itself in the knee. People always say, "Isn't running bad for your knees?". I don't necessarily believe that. However, clearly, I'm not a doctor so please don't just base your opinions on mine. However, in my journey, ALL the knee pain I had experienced while running was due to something other than my actual knee. Instead, it had been caused by my hamstrings, quads, and/or the IT band being overworked, underworked or not stretched or something similar.

God's Timing and God's Race

Sometime that September I had been getting the urge that I wanted to go back to Disney. We had skipped all of 2013 and hadn't been since February 2012. That was a LONG time. Disney withdrawal had set in badly. I had made up my mind to mention the idea of another trip to my husband. However, he was out of town and super busy, so I decided to wait until he came back and gave him some time to settle back in before I brought it up.

In the meantime, we were having our St. Jude party in the park one Saturday evening in September. As we were on our way there, Ashley called us (us being Kenzie and I) and said that she was supposed to tell us something. Greg had had a conversation with her and was giving her the privilege of passing the message on to us.

Jennifer and her family were planning a trip to Walt Disney World in December over Christmas. It was a dream of hers to go to Magic Kingdom on Christmas Day. Greg had decided that if we wanted to go, we could go again while they were going to be there. The kids always had such a great time together. He had no idea that I was planning to bring the same idea up to him only I hadn't thought enough about the when. I just wanted a trip. So, suddenly, a new Disney trip was in the works.

After having some conversations with Ashley, we both were very skeptical of the crowd levels between Christmas and New Year's. We knew enough to know that this is the busiest time of the year to go. We were leaning more towards the idea of going when the crowds were a little lighter and foregoing the opportunity to go with Jennifer and her family. Although, it was a very tough choice.

We had already experienced the Christmas decorations a couple of times. An essential piece for Ashley, however, was that she wanted to make sure she could be there the entire time this time. She was going to a junior college at the time, and the previous trip she had to come in a couple of days later because she couldn't miss that much class. We proceeded to check the calendar, researched the "crowd calendar," and checked on her college calendar. This led us to the first part of January after New Year's but before Martin Luther King Jr's Birthday because that was when she went back to school. The crowds seemed much less dramatic than the week of Christmas.

After a little further research, I realized that the week we chose fell during Marathon Weekend. My first reaction was, "Oh man. I don't know if I want to be there on a race weekend. It's probably going to be crowded, and if I'm not running in a race, I will probably be sad." This was when it all started to click. Yes, sometimes I'm a little slow. But, it finally hit me, "Hey, maybe I could do the half marathon while we were there."

Really God? Is this really happening? Are you really wanting my first half marathon to be at Disney and that it would be this trip?

Before I got too excited, we had to run the idea past Greg because we had now taken his concept and changed it dramatically since his plan was for us to go with Jennifer and her family. He was totally fine with the change if that's what we wanted to do and agreed that he wasn't going to be too crazy about the crowds and lines either.

As a bonus for us, I was able to figure out that they keep all the Christmas decorations up through the first part of January and that would mean we could experience all the Christmas fun and have fewer people to contend with.

Now, to the race. When I went to research the race, it didn't take me long to realize that the race was sold out. I have since learned that runDisney races can and often do sell out quickly and even within the first couple of days of registration opening in some cases. However, I did not know this back then. I had no clue how any of it worked given we had only done the one race there, and again I still wasn't on Facebook yet and in groups where you quickly learn this to be the norm. So, half marathon idea squashed before it even had time to start festering right? Well, not so fast.

I emailed runDisney to see what options I might have. They suggested I look into the travel agents and the charities that offer race bibs. There is a list of these on the runDisney website. I proceeded to do this and quickly realized that St. Jude Heroes is one of the charities that you can run for. Really? I just finished running for St. Jude, and it was AMAZING! Would I really have an opportunity to do this again? Could I raise that kind of money again so quickly, after all, it had just been a couple of months since I had asked for donations for the other run?

I contacted the person in charge of the St. Jude Heroes Team for this Disney race. They, unfortunately, didn't have any bibs left either. However, he said that people had to make a final decision by October, and if anyone dropped out, he would contact me. Again, half marathon idea squashed? And, again, I say, not so fast! If God wants it to happen, He will make a way even when there seems to be no way.

It would have been super easy for me to take that "injury" and all these subsequent "No's" and say, "Well, maybe this running thing isn't for me? Maybe I'm not supposed to do this race. Why would God give me this only to have it taken away so quickly?" I could've just said, "Well, that was a fun ride, but ok I guess we're on to the next thing."

Somewhere deep in my heart, I knew that wasn't true, and I knew that that was not what I was supposed to think. It wasn't even hard to convince myself to keep at it. I just had to be patient and wait for the answers to come. I knew wholeheartedly God still wanted me running. I just didn't know the specific details. Knowing that, it was super easy for me to be patient.

That is not an easy thing for me. I want to be able to fix things now, not wait. If I have a vision, I just want to grab it. I don't want to wait. With running though this was somehow easy. I was honestly never apprehensive about the "injury" being something long-term. I knew it was all part of God's plan, and when He was ready for me to move past it, He would make it happen.

Sometimes God gives us obstacles or in this case an "injury" that keep us from our plan and instead lead us on the right path for His plan. If I had not been battling that IT band issue, I absolutely would have signed up for and done the half marathon in

Springfield. With the "injury," I quickly realized that was not in the cards, so I completely dropped the idea. The entire time God was setting the stage and working out the details for the race that He wanted as my first half marathon!

So, as I continued to patiently wait to see how all of this would work out, I realized that my knee pain was resolving. I was able to start running a regular routine and started in with a solid training plan increasing my long run each week so that I could get to 12 miles before the race. I figured I needed to train just in case. The knee continued to improve as I stayed with a regular stretching routine as well. I did, however, continue to wear the knee sleeve for longer runs just for stability purposes and to play it safe.

Eventually, I got the word that someone had dropped out, and I could get in if I still wanted to. "If I wanted to? YES! OF COURSE, I WANT TO!" So, there it was. I was officially training for my first half marathon and officially raising money for St. Jude again.

Remember that dream of earning the 13.1 Mickey ears magnet for my car that I had hoped for 2013? (To be honest, I had forgotten about that dream until this all started to unfold). Well, it was going to be a year later than "my goal," but that didn't even matter. I was on my way to earning it now. The best part? It was 100% God's plan! It doesn't get any better than that!

I managed to get in the 12-miler as my longest training run before the race. I was nervous that it wasn't enough. To that point, I had always run the race distance before the race. It helped build my confidence because logically if I could do it in a training run, I could do it on race day. In this case, though, I just ran out of time and couldn't get any longer ones in. However, with the research and reading I was doing "they" say if you can do 12, then 13.1 on race day will not be an issue. I was taking "their" word for it given I had no other option at that point.

I'm so blessed to have such a supportive family, community, and group of friends. They all came through again for the children of St. Jude, and I was able to raise the amount required to participate. What an amazing opportunity! Not only was I getting ready to attempt my first half marathon, but I also was getting to run the race at Walt Disney World, AND I was getting to do it for St. Jude! Even in my wildest dreams, I couldn't have come up with such an amazingly, awesome opportunity. Shoot, I was happy with just running the half marathon in Springfield. But, WOW God, I like your plan WAY better!

Chapter Nine

Off to Walt Disney World Again

We had chosen to add Universal Studios and Islands of Adventure into this trip. We like to go there every few trips. The way our schedule was planned out, my race was at the end of the trip on Saturday, which meant we had six days in the theme parks planned before my race. In retrospect, that may not have been the best scenario for me as I was planning to run a long race.

I had once again been in charge of all the planning and making of the reservations. We had chosen a resort new to us this time, Disney's Art of Animation Resort. We all agreed on the Lion King Suite as there were 3 optional themes for the suites; Lion King, Cars, and Finding Nemo. I was super excited about the extra space we were going to have in the suite.

My in-laws were living down there for the winter again, so we had them join us at the resort. Their room was directly across the hall from ours, which made everything super easy for all of us. It was always fun when they joined us while we were there. It was like a mini vacation for them as well even though they were only about 40 minutes from their winter home.

We LOVED the resort. The themes in the rooms were amazing. No detail was left out. These suites can hold up to 6 people, so if you are a larger family or you like to spread out, this is a fantastic option. There was a bedroom with a queen bed and a bathroom with two sinks. There was a sofa bed in the living room area as well as a table that doubled as a murphy bed. This let both girls enjoy their own space and their own bed. They also had a bathroom to share with two sinks. This meant we all had our own "get ready" space that we could keep as neat and tidy or as messy as we pleased.

The extra space in these suites is unbelievable. I like to unpack and get things all in their new home so that I can be mostly organized. This helps when someone says, "Where is such and such?" I have a pretty good idea of where to search. These rooms were perfect for that.

Pre-Race

Still being the newbie to Disney races, I really had no idea what to expect. I didn't have a proof of time to submit (I didn't even know I was supposed to have one), so I was placed into corral M of corrals through P. For the half marathon you need proof of an "official" race finishing time of at least a 10K or higher to use as your proof of time.

Up to this point, I hadn't done that many actual races, just a lot of training, so, I didn't even have one to submit, even if I had wanted to. Not submitting a proof of time will get you placed in one of the last corrals. However, you can still have an amazing race starting from the back, and from what I read, there is a lot of fun to be had back there.

I should note that all this information is readily available on the runDisney website. You do not need to be on Facebook to know this, however, being new to races in general, I didn't even really understand the whole corral assignment idea fully anyways, so I certainly wasn't going to understand a proof of time. Once I was on Facebook and joined some "groups," all the logistics of it started making sense. That didn't actually happen for me until a few months down the road though.

Ashley, Kenzie, and I headed to the expo on Thursday, and again, I had no idea what to expect. When we first walked in, I remember being just completely shocked and somewhat overwhelmed. There were so many vendors, so much running stuff, and a wonderful site to look down on (You come in on the upper level. From here you get a fantastic view of all the vendors down below.)

New Balance had a huge area and some really cool Disney shoes. It seems I was probably the only person that didn't know about this ahead of time, again because I wasn't on Facebook or any social media for that matter. When I inquired about these shoes, I was told that you needed to sign up to get a spot to try them on. What? Really? And all the spots for that day had been taken. They suggested I try back the following day.

They did have some adorable Minnie Mouse shoes that were available in children's sizes. You could try on children's shoes without a time slot, just not the adult sizes. So, even though I have surprisingly large feet for my body size, I proceeded to go ahead and try them on. I tried the Minnie Mouse ones, but quickly realized they weren't the right "type" of shoe for me. The adorable

Cinderella ones, however, were. But those you needed to have a time slot for. And so, the fashion show was done for one day.

The girls and I continued exploring. We got my bib and shirt and checked out the runDisney merchandise area. They had tutus that happened to match my chosen outfit. I did know enough at that point that you aren't supposed to try anything new on race day. However, Ashley had a different idea. She kept encouraging me to get the tutu, that it would be fun. I kept trying to say no, but eventually, she won. I was pretty sure that the thing was going to be thrown to the side of the road due to it being annoying shortly into the race, and I would be out all the money I paid, but I said yes anyway.

I had unfortunately developed shin splints over the previous couple of days from all the walking around the parks. We happened to come across "the stick" vendor area. This looked interesting. It was a stick of sorts that you roll over your muscles. I told one of the sales reps about my shin splints. She informed me that this was generating from my calves - had no idea. (Looking back, I sometimes wonder how I managed through all this stuff with my complete lack of knowledge, but I did.) She proceeded to roll out my calves with "the stick." Wow! What a difference! I was sold! Off we went with all our goodies and headed back to the resort to meet everyone else.

We chose to change the plan slightly and take it easy and relax a little on Friday and just see how the day went. This opened the door for me to head back to the expo and try my luck with the queue for the Cinderella shoes. I was able to get in the queue and was told it would probably be an hour and a half or so wait.

I continued exploring the expo while I waited. There was no need to sit by and watch anxiously as the individuals before me on the list tried on the long-awaited shoes. The system they had was so high-tech that they sent out a text alert when it was finally your turn. So, it didn't matter where you were, you wouldn't miss the notification. The moment came, and I received my text that it was my turn. Hooray!

I tried them on and was instantly in love. They were so adorable. There was no way I could leave without them. I have worn those shoes a ton over the last four years. I have definitely gotten my money's worth out of them. In fact, I found them to be so comfortable that I bought the same shoe in a basic design without Cinderella on them as my new, daily running shoes. I have stuck with that same shoe ever since. I have upgraded to the newer model when it came out, but otherwise, it's still my favorite. They were totally worth every second of the wait to try them out.

Chapter Ten

It's RACE DAY

If you have ever been to theme parks, you know they can be exhausting. I was exhausted. My legs and feet were so sore every single night when I went to bed and were only mildly better by morning. I kept thinking to myself. "How in the world are you going to run 13.1 miles?" Sleep was also at a minimum because we went to bed late and got up early. But, I kept going. There was so much fun to be had and so many things to experience. Our family 's motto at Disney is always "we can sleep when we get home." So, I am not complaining one bit! I was just wondering how the 13.1 miles would actually fit into that schedule.

It was finally Saturday and race day. I'm one that likes to get to the race area early, and by early, I mean super early. I want to make sure I'm there and get my bearings, so to speak. The race started at 5:30, but I think I got up at 2:00 am to start my getting ready process. (The races need to start super early so most of the runners can be finished before the parks open.) I had brought an instant oatmeal packet and ate that before I left the room. Again, my stomach is very touchy on what works and doesn't work when I run, and I knew better than to try something new, so I planned ahead and brought what I knew would be ok from home. The room had a microwave, so this was an easy thing to prepare.

Kenzie wanted to do my hair for me. I woke her up, so she could do that with her eyes barely open. We had found a princess bow to put in with my ponytail. We weren't putting together a "costume," but it was a Disney race and I wanted to have a little fun with my appearance. She took a few pictures for me in the hallway and back to bed she went. I was off to the bus.

I had a hand-held water bottle I started carrying with me for hydration on my training runs, and I had brought a breakfast bar of some sort to try and munch on way before the race. I was worried about getting hungry and not having enough energy for the race, especially since I had left so early.

I arrived at the "staging area" with plenty of time to chill and wait. The "staging area" at a Disney race is a HUGE area where they have a few booths, water stations, porta-potties, music, lights, characters, etc. This is where everyone waits before it's time to start heading to the corrals. Again, being new to this whole experience, I didn't know what I was supposed to be doing, so I just found a spot, sat down, and started watching people. I snacked on a little of my bar as I waited. Finally, they announced it was time that we could start heading to our corrals.

Ok, progress, this was good! I got up and followed the crowd. I had seen a picture of how the corrals were set up, but still really had no idea what all this meant. I also had no idea that the corrals were so far away from the staging area. I didn't track it, but it seemed like a really long walk. I finally could see the huge, lit-up balloons with letters signifying the corrals and headed toward corral M. I secured a spot in the corral and proceeded to wait. I saw others sitting, so I decided to sit and chill again. I'm not sure how long this was, but it too seemed like forever.

There was, of course, lots of Disney fun to entertain us. HUGE screens were broadcasting a feed from the starting line. Speakers, interviews, songs, and games were going on to keep us pumped up and ready to run.

Eventually, it was time for the first corral to begin. This was the wheelchair division. We could see the starting line on the screen, and the countdown began. Fireworks were the mark of the start for them. It had officially started! Now, to wait my turn. A few minutes later the next corral was ready to go, and the countdown was beginning. And much to my surprise, fireworks again! I remember thinking, "Seriously? We ALL get fireworks? How cool is that?" This gave each corral the feeling of the same importance as the first corral. A great and appreciated detail on runDisney's planning side.

The corrals were released one at a time. I had no idea how long it would take for my corral to begin, so I just kept patiently waiting and slowly moving forward with the rest of my fellow corral M people. The race started at 5:30 am, and my corral finally began at 6:20 am.

Off we went. I had finally started running. I had officially started my first half marathon and had officially begun the 13.1-mile journey to the finish line, not having any idea what was in store ahead. One detail I did know was that we got to run through the castle! I was looking very forward to that of course.

I was not anticipating how crowded it would be at the beginning. We had two lanes of road and two shoulders, but it was still packed. I went against all my sense of logic and joined the people in the grass on the right. As I was doing it, I knew it was a bad idea. I even kept telling myself that, but I had to get around those people somehow so that I could hold a steady pace. I knew that I was risking a severe ankle injury on the uneven ground, and the grass was harder work for my legs than the pavement, but I needed to get to what I was used to, so I ran out there until things spread out a little more.

Suddenly everyone started cheering and yelling. I quickly glanced around to see what was happening. The lead runners were on the other side of the road on their way back and headed towards the finish line. How exciting for them! I was sincerely excited for them but at the same time the "Aw man, they are almost finished, and I'm only about a mile and a half into this thing" came into my head. I put that out of my head, refocused on the music, and just ran.

Before I made it to Magic Kingdom, I was probably at about mile 4-ish and felt as though I was really struggling. It was quite frustrating to me because I had no idea why I would be struggling at this point. I had run MANY training runs longer than 4 miles, and I had to get to 13, so struggling at 4 was not a good sign.

There is a bridge over the road in this area close to Magic Kingdom. In fact, above the road is water. Yes, we got to run underneath the water. That little fun fact is still pretty cool. Standing on the bridge was a DJ playing music and shouting and cheering. He had a HUGE Mickey hand glove he was waving to all of us. This was certainly a much-appreciated perk at that point. As you go under the bridge, however, you go down a hill. In reality, it's not a big hill. But, in my running reality, it was a significant hill. I was quickly concerned about now having to go back up. Well, then it was confirmed, yes on the other side of the bridge we have to go back up.

Head down, one step at a time I did that hill. I survived. If any of you reading this know the area I'm referring to, you are probably laughing at me about now as I gripe about this "hill." I get it, but we have already established that hills, even the small ones, and I, don't see eye to eye.

Now, it's getting fun as we have gotten to the Contemporary Resort area and can see the entrance to Magic Kingdom. We didn't go through the regular entrance. Instead, we came in through a backstage area. I knew Main Street, U.S.A. and Cinderella Castle were coming up very soon. This would help me feel better, and oh boy did it! As a Disney fan, Main Street, U.S.A. brings tears to my eyes every time. But this time, I was getting to run up it! WOW! How incredibly awesome! People were lining the edges high-fiving and cheering. There were tons of signs and support. It truly was amazing!

Up ahead there it was, Cinderella Castle! It's so beautiful! By this point, the sun had come up enough that you couldn't tell that it was still lit up for Christmas, but that didn't matter. It was still a perfectly magical moment. I was running a race through Magic Kingdom. Even now as I type this many years later, it still seems almost unreal, but it was definitely real.

The course turns you to the right and into Tomorrowland. We looped around to then come through the castle through the back. There it was, I was running through Cinderella Castle! Words cannot describe what an incredible feeling that was.

From a running perspective though, it can get very congested in here with runners, as its much narrower than the other areas. We took a sharp turn after the castle and headed towards Adventureland. Eventually, you cross the railroad tracks and head backstage.

Backstage is the official Disney word for the "behind the scenes" type areas. This whole concept is fantastic to me, but that's a whole other story. There were a few of the parade floats out for us with princesses and princes waving and ready for pictures. One of the perks of Disney races are the character stop photo opportunities along the courses. Many runners stop and get photos with some of their favorite characters. In fact, races are a great opportunity to see some of the characters that you can't generally find in the parks on a daily basis. I didn't stop for photos, but it was great to see as I ran past. My goal was to run every step of this race, so I couldn't stop for any photos.

Quickly we were back out on the road and headed back towards Epcot, where we started. I was again feeling the struggle and again so frustrated as to why. I slowly sipped on my water but wanted to make sure it lasted through the race. I'm not a stop at water stops kind of person as the one time I tried I slopped the water all over myself as I tried to drink and run at the same time.

There were more bands, character stops, and cheering sections on the roads to try and keep us excited and to add to the magic of running at Disney World. That is such a perk to Disney races.

Around mile 9 or 10 or so I could see an overpass. It was packed with runners. I was extremely puzzled, and I think slightly delusional. I wondered was there another race going on? Who were those runners and why were they up there? It truly is comical looking back on it after the fact. It didn't take me too long to realize that, no... those runners were running the same race as me, and I was going to have to become one of them. Now, the real question. I know you all know exactly where I'm heading with this. How in the world do I get up there? Is there some sort of elevator-type thing that is going to carry us up there? (Yes, that thought did actually go through my head. Again, likely delusion from dehydration.)

And then I could see it... the on-ramp! Yes, an on-ramp, like on the highway when you exit the highway and you go up one of those half circle on/off ramps... we had to run up that thing to get on the bridge! "Oh my! This is HORRIBLE! It's so long and so steep. There is no way I can run up this thing. But, I have to." So, again head down, and as much to the inside corner as I could get (because clearly, that's the shortest distance to the top) I focused on 1 step at a time up the ramp. I did make it up the ramp continuing to run the whole time. YES! Mission accomplished!

Ok, we should be fine now, right? Nope. About another mile or so later there was another hill/ramp. Seriously? Who designed this course? Who puts these at the end of the course? This was clearly just my fatigue and sassy side coming out. About halfway up the hill, I remember feeling like I absolutely couldn't go any further and that I could pass out. I prayed for God to please give me the strength to keep going, to help me get up that hill and ultimately be able to finish that race. At that moment, I felt like I was lifted. I didn't come off the ground, but I could feel something helping me stay upright and helping me to continue moving forward. Thank you, God!

I had come so far. He had given me the gift of doing this race. I had trained as hard as I could, and there was no way I was going to give up now. Someone was going to have to pick me up off the ground because I passed out before I gave up. I was going to do every step of it running no matter what. So, I kept going slow and steady. I had since finished all the water in my bottle and was getting quite thirsty but only had a mile or 2 to go so surely, I would be fine.

Eventually, we made it to the parking lot outside Epcot. Again, a ton of wonderful people lining the ropes that blocked off the course. Hundreds of signs with encouraging words. Thank you to all for those perfect strangers. I know I have said it before, but the importance of this cannot be understated. Just the smallest little smile, sign, high five, etc. can make the difference between continuing or stopping.

I made it into Epcot, finally. Almost there! We could see the guests at the entrance to the park as this was now shortly before 9:00 am when the park was set to open. They too were cheering and clapping. What a sight! Did they know that they were going to get to see us when they made their plans to open Epcot that day? I don't know the answer to that obviously, but I was sure happy to see them even though they were all strangers.

Up the hill at Spaceship Earth (notice I'm not complaining about this hill), I passed the fountain, and headed towards the World Showcase to the turn-around and back towards Spaceship Earth. I turned the corner at Spaceship Earth to head backstage. I was getting so close and could barely keep moving forward.

The 13-mile marker, I could see it!! Only .1 to go! Of course, my phone told me I was done a long time ago, but we can't go by that. Then I heard the Gospel Choir. I don't know if they were affiliated with Disney or a local church, but they were AMAZING! They were dressed all in their robes (they had to be incredibly hot) and just singing beautifully for us. That brings tears to your eyes. It's one of the true highlights of the race. They were so special and perfectly placed at the end of the race. I just cannot tell you how incredible they are, how beautifully they sing, and how wonderful it is to see and hear them!

I could finally see the end! There were crowds on the left. I tried to glance to see if I could see my family, but I couldn't. I couldn't move my head to try and scan the crowd. I was afraid that anything other than straightforward motion and vision would cause me to fall because I was so exhausted. But, I did at least try to see them. I was close to the finish line. It was really going to happen. I saw Donald Duck over on the right near the finish line, but I was on the left. I honestly had nothing left to be able to take the diagonal and head towards him. I needed to take as few steps as possible and just finish. I wanted to put my arms up, but even they were exhausted. They only went about halfway. I finished!

I had really done it! Then I looked up and just on the other side of the fencing structure was my family! I was so happy to see them! Greg, Ashley, Kenzie, and my father-in-law. They were all there! If I didn't already have tears from finishing, they were fully flowing now.

I had to continue through the finishing area and would meet them on the other side as they aren't allowed in that area with the runners. I was still crying when I got my medal, of course. I grabbed a couple of Gatorades, a bottle of water, and of course the famous runDisney snack box and banana. (Some claim to run the races just to receive those.)

All I was focused on at that point was getting through all of this to get back to my family. But, I did remember that I was thirsty, so I started drinking. Ok, chugging the Gatorade was a better description of what I did. I finally made it to the other side and was reunited with my people/my family!

Chapter Eleven

I'm going to back up now a little and cover some 'backstory" for you.

We had been eating lunch a few days before the race at one of our favorite restaurants at Hollywood Studios, the 50's Prime Time Café, and were fortunate enough that our favorite server was working and was available to be our server. It turns out that he was also a runner. Since he lives and works there, he had participated in quite a few runDisney races and was quite experienced with the course, the process, and the logistics. He sat and chatted with us through nearly the entire meal.

He led us to a couple of apps for our phones that would allow my family to track me. Remember, this was back in 2014. Smartphones weren't new, but they were new enough that not everyone, including us, knew that things like this existed. We did manage to set this up on our phones and even tested it out to make sure it was working. This was great! Now they would be able to follow me, see me progress, and know when I was getting ready to finish.

My mother-in-law had terrible knees at this point. She planned to get them both replaced as soon as they returned to Illinois in the spring. Due to her knees, she was unable to stand or walk for even a short period without pain. So, rather than her standing around for a long time (which she was not able to do anyway), it was decided that she would wait at the resort until she knew I had finished and then head to meet us at Hollywood Studios where we planned to spend the rest of the day.

Kenzie had brought her iPad with her, and since we were now all linked into Find My Phone, we were also able to connect the iPad. This was fantastic! It allowed my mother-in-law to track me as well. I know that she so desperately wanted to be there to see me finish, but she just was not physically able at that point to do so.

She was overjoyed that she could still see me as I traveled my 13.1-mile distance. She took countless screenshots that she sent to me later and my husband as he was waiting. I'm not sure if she realized he saw the same information on his phone, but it was still awesome. She too was right there cheering for me even though she was doing it from the resort room.

This was how they were able to know precisely when I was going to finish and how they knew when to slide to that spot at the finish line. If not for all that, and their quick thinking, I would not have that fantastic memory to cherish forever! Again, thank you God for guiding us to each and every one of these specific details that all fell perfectly into place!

Remember during the 5K how I wondered how in the world we found each other? Well, thanks to technology we now had a solution for that, and it could not have worked more perfectly in this situation.

Back to the post-race happenings - I was hurting. I was exhausted. I was starving. I was thirsty. But, I was so happy to see them and give hugs all around. I of course still had tears when I saw them. It was like my body just knew, ok now you can let go. I told them it was absolutely the hardest thing I had ever done.

I cannot tell you how wonderful it is that my daughters both got to see me finish. They saw me set a goal, train hard, and then ultimately complete that goal. This was not something they got to see me do on a regular basis as this was pretty foreign for me at that point.

I had given every ounce of everything I had inside me to complete that race - physically, mentally, emotionally, everything. I had worked so hard for that and stretched myself beyond all measures I could've ever anticipated. I did it, and I didn't give up. I didn't give in to all the negatives hitting me. I remained focused on the fact that this was not my race. This was God's race. He wanted me there. He put me there. He wanted me to run it. He had helped me train hard for it and had helped me prepare for it.

With Him, I can do all things - including this. That was what got me to that finish line. Sure, He had blessed me with the opportunity to do all of this at Disney, but ultimately it was still His race and His journey for me. I can still remember the moment on that hill around mile 11 when I was sure that I was going to collapse to the ground, but that instead, He lifted me up and carried me the rest of the way to finish that race. He is so so good!

Remember the Gatorade chugging I mentioned? That was not one of my wisest choices. I quickly realized that it was way too early to try that. It almost immediately made my stomach a mess. Off to the bathroom I went. My family was so patient as we tried to make the walk over to the main Epcot parking lot to jump on a bus to Hollywood Studios. It was quite a bit of a walk, and I was pretty slow. They let me take as much time as I needed and let me stop at as many porta potties as I needed. We eventually made it onto a bus and were headed to Hollywood Studios. At that point, I was feeling much better and was all smiles, wearing my medal proudly, and starting to tell them all the stories, experiences, and adventures I had just encountered over the last 2 and a half hours.

The following day we had to return home. This is always a sad day for us. In fact, the bus transportation that takes us to and from the airport to our Disney resort is called Magical Express. However, when we are returning to the airport to head home, we have nicknamed it the "Tragical Express". There was a marathon that morning as the final race of the weekend. After my half and how tough that was, I could not possibly imagine how people were able to run twice that far.

We didn't have to leave until later in the day and were able to see some of the marathon runners at the resort. They were very easy to spot either by their beautiful medal/medals or by the hobbling or the ice bags wrapped around their knees. We did get the opportunity to speak with some of these runners. Surprisingly they said that the marathon was easier than the half marathon. What? How in the world was that possible? But, that did make me feel somewhat better as I still had no idea why I struggled so badly on the half. I naturally didn't expect it to be easy, but the fact that I was struggling from mile 4 on really confused me as I should've been comfortable still at that point. After all, 4 miles had become a pretty easy distance for me.

I eventually started putting the pieces together. Apparently, on the day of the half, Orlando broke a record for heat and humidity. So, it was extremely humid and hot while we were running. Ah, now it's making sense. Humidity seems to suck your breath right out of you. It's almost like you can hardly breathe. At that point in

84

my training, though, I couldn't tell all that. Now, I can get a few houses down the road and know whether it's humid or not, sometimes it doesn't even take that long. Also, keep in mind I was again training in Illinois in the winter. Heat and humidity were the opposite of my most recent training conditions.

I also started looking at the timing of it all. There was a very long time that I was waiting to start running. It was over 4 hours from the time I got up until the time I started running. I had eaten more than three hours before starting the race, so that wasn't doing me a lot of good by race time. And, with the high humidity, I needed to drink a lot more than my one 16 oz water bottle over that period. I was starving and VERY thirsty when I finished. Both contribute significantly to how you feel while running and lacking in either or both can make a run downright horrible.

I had been concerned because I thought it was just my training, that I hadn't worked hard enough. Sure, there is always room for improvement there, but I had been good about not skipping runs and sticking to the plan. It was all starting to make sense now. The temperature, the humidity, my lack of understanding the logistics of the race, my lack of fueling while running, and my not having enough water during the run all combined to make the run the difficulty level that it turned out to be. Again, don't get me wrong, I did not expect a half marathon to be easy, but it should've been more comfortable than it was.

The bright side is there were once again many lessons to learn from this. Moving forward, I was going to learn to fuel while I ran. This in and of itself was going to be a battle since my stomach was so sensitive while I'm running, but it was required if I wanted to continue with longer distances. I also needed to incorporate more water.

I also decided that if I was ever going to do another runDisney half marathon that I was going to have a proof of time to submit for better corral placement. I had no idea that I would have to wait 50 minutes from the time the race started until I got to run. I mean, looking back, it seems obvious. To get 25,000 runners started, you obviously must space them out somehow. Again, at that point, my lack of experience with something like this just meant I really didn't have any grasp on how this all could work. So, my advice to anyone is to try and get a proof of time if you can. There is also an issue of the time requirements for completing the race and the balloon ladies, but I'll get to that later.

Chapter Twelve

Spring 2014

Anew race was now on my radar. This time it was a local one. This event included a half marathon, a marathon, and a marathon relay as some of their race opportunities. It was being held on a Sunday morning and started and ended in downtown Peoria. This required many of the streets to be closed in the area. That was going to be an issue for our church since it is located right where the race was being held. As a result, our church decided we could not have Sunday morning services that day and planned to reschedule services for a later time. This opened up my Sunday morning and the idea that maybe I should consider participating.

Our church was trying to "Go" and "occupy every street in the city of Peoria." I thought what better way to do that than to run one of these races with my "church race shirt" as I had affectionately named it. I was torn between the half marathon and the marathon relay. I had never done a relay and thought that if I could gather up three other ladies from our church to run the other legs, it would be a super fun event for all of us.

I wasn't very connected with other people at the church, so this was going to prove somewhat challenging. I was willing to at least try. My fallback if I couldn't find a team was to do the half marathon on my own. I was training to do the 15K Steamboat Race anyway, so I had kept my mileage at a decent level.

I found two other ladies easily, but we still needed a fourth. We were coming up to the final weeks prior to the race and we still hadn't found a 4th. I just kept praying, "God I really feel like you want this to happen. If so, please guide us to the 4th person to fill our team." Sure enough, just when I had almost lost all hope of the relay, He provided our 4th. Again, I just needed to have faith and patiently wait for Him to show the plan. We managed to get a church shirt for each of us so that for every step of the race, whoever was around us would know we were there and more importantly that God was there.

I chose to run the second leg because I thought my St. Jude team was going to be operating a water station in that section. However, unbeknownst to me, they had been switched to mile 19 or somewhere in that range. The second leg also meant that I would run up the Main Street hill. (If you are from the area, you know exactly what this means.) This is a long and steep hill, and well, we have already discussed how much I dislike hills, but I was willing to do it. As I look back, that hill didn't seem all that horrible. I just kept moving forward. Our first runner was fast, so a lot of fast runners now surrounded me. I think they helped me pick up a pace that was a bit faster than I had thought I could do, but it felt comfortable, so I stayed with it.

We had once again used technology to link up our phones with each other, so the other three members would know where we were and when to be ready for the handoff. We had a general idea of pace, and how long it "should" take, but in my case, for example, I was running about 30-45 seconds per mile faster than I told them, so it was good that they were tracking me.

On this journey, I wanted to spend my time praying for the people in the race, the people that lived in the houses I passed, and the people that were out cheering us on or volunteering. This was so very special to me. I enjoyed every step of my 6+ mile portion of that marathon.

I made the handoff to our next runner, and she was off. This was a fantastic experience. Since I had never experienced a marathon relay before, I had no idea what to expect. The whole process was just so exciting and fun. On the last leg, we had decided that the 3 of us would catch up with our final runner at our church, as it was located near the end of the race.

In the relay, they let the team finish together. We just planned to converge a little earlier than they scheduled it. We finished together, and we finished strong. What a fantastic opportunity that, again, I will cherish forever. The ladies were so kind to let me keep our baton since it was my idea to do it, and I proudly have that in my display with the rest of my race bibs and medals.

Once we finished and could talk about our experience, we learned that our last runner had a great experience on her leg. There was another runner near her that was doing the marathon with either her friend or sister. She was struggling greatly and was ready to quit. Our runner was able to talk with her and pray over her. They were so grateful to her for that gesture, and she was able to finish the race on her own. If hers was the only life we touched that day, it was worth it. We had done what I had hoped we could accomplish. We showed 26.2 miles of Peoria who Jesus is!

It also turned out that the races were supporting the St. Jude runs. So, it was a win all around for everyone!

Chapter Thirteen

Let's talk about the training

I think it's clear that, for me, this running thing has nothing to do with losing weight or staying in shape. However, those have been definite perks along the way. If only I would make better food choices...

Anyway, all my training is done on the streets of Wyoming, or probably 98% of it. I feel so welcomed and so comfortable here. I have routes that I like for certain distances, but I do like to change it up a little here and there. Since I usually run alone, I stay in town and not far from someone or someplace I know. I always have a plan on where I can go if I have trouble. I have learned where every dog is on my routes and which ones have an electric fence, which ones are on a chain and how far that chain goes, and which ones are loose.

Everyone is wonderful here. I get a wave from almost every person I pass whether they are in a car or in their yard. I feel confident that I could reach out to nearly every person/house if I needed help. I feel like they have gotten used to me running around town after all these years. They watch for me. When they see me out and about, they will say, "Hey I saw you running the other day." "How's your running going?" "When's your next race?" This is one of the beautiful things about living in such a small community and a wonderful town. I'm so blessed to have this as my training ground.

As another perk, while I'm running, I can pray for them. I don't know everyone, but that doesn't matter. I can still pray for blessings in their lives and for God to make a difference for them. Some I do know, and I know of hardships, struggles, and difficulties, and I pray for them in those areas. I pray for the town itself. I honestly cannot put into words how great of a gift it is to be running through this town all these years.

My training is more than just exercise. Since I only listen to Christian music while I run, the lyrics can sink fully into my heart. This is my time with God. Running alone gives me the opportunity to connect with Him. He speaks to me on these runs. I put the music on shuffle, and often I realize the specific songs He chose that day were significant in the message He wanted for me at that moment. He nudges me. He guides me. When I have challenging decisions that I'm just not sure how to make, He gives me the answers clearly on these runs. It's our connecting place. It's almost like I have my very own church service with my runs. This doesn't happen on every run, but that doesn't make those runs any less important. I still need to be out there running.

He has pushed me to distances I never dreamt of. He took pains away in the middle of runs so that I could complete the mileage I had set out for. He has even changed the weather so that it was not horrible when I needed to run. I'm so grateful for all of this and that I am able to recognize His hand in all of it. It reinforces that this is EXACTLY what He wants me doing!

Facebook

I finally joined the world of Facebook earlier this year (2014). I had started as a Pampered Chef consultant, and as a Marketing major, it was apparent this would be a great tool to get the word out about my new business. This also opened the door for me to start joining some running and Disney groups. Now I was really starting to learn. I was learning about running. I was learning about Disney. And, I was learning about running at Disney.

Thanksgiving 2014 - Jennifer and I came up with the great idea to try and train for and complete the runDisney Coast-to-Coast Challenge in 2016. The Coast-to-Coast Challenge is when you run a half marathon or the marathon at Walt Disney World and a half marathon at Disneyland in the same calendar year. Not only would you earn the medals from each race, but you also then earn the special Coast-to-Coast medal. We wanted to take this one step further and earn the pink Coast-to-Coast medal because, well, pink is an awesome color. The normal medal was blue. They were the same medal- one was pink, and one was blue. To earn the pink Coast-to-Coast medal, you needed to complete the Princess Half Marathon in February at Walt Disney World and the Tinker Bell Half Marathon in May at Disneyland.

We decided that it would be fun to invite others to do this with us if they wanted to. This was how our Facebook group was formed. We created a group that would allow people to not just join us on this adventure, but also have a safe place to share workouts, struggles, nutrition, and to hold one another accountable. We wanted to encourage as many people as we could to get moving.

If they wanted to try and join us for the races, they had almost 1-½ years to train. This is generally plenty of time to work up to that distance, although it obviously took me a little longer. We wanted people to dream and to dream big. Why not? You won't push yourself to do the unimaginable if you don't first set a goal to do the unimaginable. We have had quite a few family members and friends join our little group since we started it, and we have been encouraging and helping each other ever since.

At some point, we decided to up the game a little and added the challenges. For the Princess Half Marathon Weekend, we added the Glass Slipper Challenge which is the 10K on Saturday and the half marathon on Sunday for a total of 19.3 miles in 2 days. For the Tinker Bell Half Marathon Weekend, it was called the Pixie Dust Challenge. The same schedule and the same distances just in California instead of Florida. This seemed like an impossible task for both of us when we decided on it, but again set your dreams big or you can't possibly expect to do big things.

Chapter Fourteen

Stephanie

The fall of 2015 is when God blessed me with Stephanie. She and David had started dating. When he told me she was a runner I was super excited. However, she had done a couple of marathons at this point, so she was a "real" runner… much more advanced than my total amateur status. If I'm honest, I was a bit intimidated because I didn't think I knew much about running, but I was so excited to have something in common with her.

David knew we had these races planned, and he liked Disney, so he suggested that they come with us and that Steph could run with us. What a wonderful idea. However, the Princess races were sold out at that point.

Those races can sell out literally within hours of registration opening. I quickly started doing some research in my groups to see if there was some other option. I was led again back to the list of charities and travel agents that had bibs. We were late to the game on doing fundraising for a charity, so I decided to pursue the travel agent avenue. I was able to find one that still had challenge bibs available, so we got her all signed up and ready to go.

Glass Slipper Challenge training

Somewhere amid the plan for the Coast-to-Coast, the Disneyland part of the plan became a huge question mark. Jennifer had decided that she couldn't do it as she had too many other commitments and responsibilities that she just had to back out. I still had it in my head that I really wanted to earn that pink Coast-to-Coast medal but going to California was a much more expensive adventure than Florida, even though it would just be for a long weekend.

Although I hadn't given up on the idea by any means, it had been pushed to the side a little with no real guarantees that it could happen. It was in God's hands. I knew if He wanted it to happen, He would make it clear that I was supposed to do it and guide the path to making it happen. And, if not, well that was totally ok too. Disappointing but ok, because His plan is so much greater than mine.

I decided to try the Jeff Galloway training plan designed for this challenge. He is the training guy for runDisney races. There are specific training plans that he has created for each race/challenge posted on the runDisney website. I had started two weeks earlier than it called for as I was new to official training plans and wanted to allow some room in case of unforeseen issues. I wanted to make sure I got all the training in, and things always come up, so I figured a 2-week buffer was a great idea.

I managed to stick to the plan extremely well. I even found that I was getting a little faster. This was despite the fact that, again, I live in Illinois and training outside in the winter can be challenging to say the least. Cold, wind, ice, snow, dark, you name it, they all play a role in trying to get those training runs in. I was not used to running back-to-back days anymore. After the first year, I went to 3 runs per week. However, since this challenge consisted of a 10K followed by the half marathon the next day, it was essential that I train for that. As I've mentioned, I'm not the kind of a runner that can go out and "wing it." I, therefore, needed to prepare for the mileage and the actual race simulation.

Once I got to the weeks where I was doing the same distance as the races and realized that my times were better than when I had run the half at Disney in 2014, I was excited. I mean this was not just a half. This had a 10K the day before, which is a whole new ballgame. One would assume you would be slower due to the higher mileage, right?

I was now starting to think that maybe I could not just conquer this challenge but that I could PR (personal record) the half as well. What? Really? Back-to-back races and a PR? Could that be possible? Naturally, as a runner, you hope to get stronger and maybe even a little faster as you continue to train. I started this running thing at 40, so I didn't have high hopes of becoming a major speedster.

I didn't focus on this with actual speed work and weightlifting or anything. It was just the consistency, increase in mileage, and stretching that were all helping to get me stronger and a little faster. Keep in mind I was also training solo. It is difficult to push for speed when you are training alone.

This little PR goal/hope I had for myself didn't last long. About a week or 2 before we were set to leave, I started getting these feelings. Remember how Jennifer was doing the race too? Well, her schedule was crazy at the time. She worked full-time. Nicole was in her senior year of high school and was a cheerleader, so there were countless basketball games all over the place. Plus, it gets dark at 4:00, and she lives in the country. Training was extremely challenging for her. There was just not enough time to fit it all in. I know we can all relate to that. She trained as much as her schedule would allow, but she didn't feel overly confident about the race. These "feelings," "nudges," whatever you want to call them, kept telling me to run it with her. I mean, we were running it together because we were running the same race. However, we hadn't planned to run it side by side.

I knew she could do it on her own. I absolutely had no doubt. However, she had concerns. There was also the issue of the balloon ladies. (Remember I mentioned them earlier and said we would come back to this? Well, here it is). I assume this is not uniquely a Disney thing, but there are a few people that act as unofficial pacers. In this case, they have balloons tied to them, so they are easy to spot. In a Disney race, you must maintain a 16 minute per mile pace. This pace is set by the balloon ladies who are the last people to start the race. So, however far in front of them you start gives you a certain amount of cushion or buffer. Then, if you can run faster than a 16 minute per mile pace you gain even more of a cushion on top of that. If you do fall behind the balloon ladies, you run the risk of being swept. This means they have you leave the course and they shuttle you back to the finish line. I knew that unless something went horribly wrong for her, which obviously you hope won't, she would be able to finish without risk of being swept. However, the nudges were persistent.

I knew these were God nudges. They were too obvious not to be. So, I knew it was what He wanted me to do, and therefore it was the way I needed to run this race. After all, if not for Him, I wouldn't even be doing the race at all. So, I quickly gave up that idea of a PR on this half and went with God's nudges instead. I was absolutely okay with that.

You are probably thinking something like, "Yeah, well it's ok, there's probably another race you can PR at." And, yes, I'm sure there probably was or would be, but at that point, I didn't have any other races planned. I really don't run a lot of races locally. I run a couple of significant ones to my journey, and I ran a couple of Disney races. Otherwise, there just really wasn't a lot of races in my schedule. And, again although I was still hoping that by some miracle the Coast-to-Coast would happen, it was now February, and that was in May, and it just did not look feasible at all. None of that mattered though. It didn't matter what I thought I wanted for the race or how I thought the race was going to go. What mattered was running the races that God wanted me to run. This running journey is all for Him, and I want to run it the way He tells me to.

So, this was the new plan. I was going to run it with Jennifer. I wasn't sure how she was going to feel about it, but I knew that was what God wanted and therefore exactly what I was going to do. When I ran the plan past Jennifer and asked if she'd mind me running with her, she agreed, but insisted that I didn't need to do that. She was concerned she would slow me down, and that I should go at my own pace. I explained that this was God's decision not mine and I wanted to run it with her. I assured her that the speed didn't matter. God wanted us to experience it together, and if she needed me to help keep her pushing, I was there for encouragement. Again, I knew she could do it whether I was there or not, but sometimes it's helpful to have that buddy that you know you can count on.

Chapter Fifteen

It's time to head to Disney

The long-awaited race weekend arrived. Stephanie and I were signed up for the challenge, Jennifer was doing the half, and Kenzie was doing the 10K. Ashley, Kenzie, and I arrived on the Tuesday before so that we could enjoy a little more Disney time on our race-cation (race vacation).

Unfortunately, late Wednesday night Kenzie came down with some stomach thing, we still don't know what it was, but she was up much of the night with her "symptoms." This was quite troublesome since she was signed up for the 10K on Saturday.

We went to the expo that day to get all our gear. She barely made it, given her ill and dehydrated state. Friday, I tried to get her to fuel and hydrate, but she still wasn't close to 100%, so nothing sounded good. We did the best we could. This was not how she had hoped to go into her first ever 10K, but she insisted on doing it.

It's RACE DAY

We had made matching Elsa (from the movie *Frozen*) costumes, so we had already planned to stay together during the race. This illness ensured that momma was going to stay right by her side in case she had any issues. She, of course, said she would be fine, but I had to make sure for myself.

The 3 of us started the race together. This was basically Stephanie's first experience with Disney (she had been a LONG time ago but didn't remember it). It was also, therefore, her first runDisney race! How exciting. I LOVE experiencing Disney with someone for the first time! A fantastic opportunity if you are a Disney fan, one I highly recommend.

Anyway, off we went slow and steady. We got about a mile or 2 in, and Kenzie started feeling bad and needed to rest. We let Steph go on ahead because we didn't know what we were in store for and what Kenzie could handle. I knew she was dehydrated because she had eliminated everything from her system and hadn't been able to replenish what she had lost.

We stopped on the side of the course for a few minutes to try and let her body settle. A wonderful runner stopped to see if we were ok. I explained that she had had the flu and was having some dehydration issues. She cautioned against drinking too much water as that can be just as detrimental when trying to run. She had a package of apples that she gave to Kenzie to see if that would help settle her stomach.

This is where it gets funny! Me, the mom, the protector, the one that is supposed to be taking care of her daughter lets her take food from a stranger! Yep, I did that, and I didn't even have one thought about how wrong that could be. Then, there is the fact we're at Disney running a princess-inspired race, and it's an apple no less.

Is anyone thinking of the story of Snow White and her poison apple about now? Yep, I did that!

Eventually, probably after telling the story to clear-minded adults, it finally hit me that this was an epic Mom fail. However, obviously it was not a poisonous apple, and the lady was very sweet! I'm super appreciative that she was there to help. This was a reminder that there are great people in the world that are willing to help perfect strangers. This is something we see all the time during races. Runners are an incredible group of people. Later, when we were back at the resort food court, Kenzie showed me the package of apples in the case exactly like the one the lady gave her and said, "See Mom, I told you it was fine!" We still crack up at the memory of this.

Back to the race. She was able to continue, but we had to take it slow. She kept telling me she was fine and that I could leave her, but I absolutely wasn't doing that. I was probably driving her crazy though with my, "Are you ok?".

The 10K course goes around the Boardwalk Resort area between Epcot and Hollywood Studios. It is a nice loop around the lake. On Friday we were at Epcot and wanted to park hop to Hollywood Studios. We just missed the boat literally, and it was going to be another half hour or so before the next one came.

The nice gentleman at the dock informed us that it was maybe a little more than a mile walk to Hollywood Studios, perhaps a mile and a half. Clearly, we could walk that in less than a half an hour. However, remember we have two races to run and 19.3 miles to cover, so we are supposed to be "resting' and "taking it easy." I have decided that I am not capable of either of those at Disney.

The rest of our party said, "It's up to you guys (Steph and I). What do you want to do... walk or wait, you guys are the ones that have to run?" We decided to go ahead and walk. What's another mile or 2, right?

When we got to the Boardwalk area during the race, I thought Kenzie might kill me. She was like "What? Do we have to go all the way around this? I thought we were almost done!" Had we not walked it the day before she would have had no idea what to expect, but in her ill state this seemed like 100 miles instead of just a few (because we still had to loop around the whole other side of the lake not just to Hollywood Studios). She stuck with it though.

We stopped for some convenient pics that doubled as a nice little rest for her body, and we otherwise kept moving forward. We saw the same nice lady that gave her the apples a few more times before we finished which was a pleasant surprise.

The finish line was finally in sight. We crossed with no significant mishaps. When we returned to the resort, she was able to take a short nap, and then was ready to start building back up her water and food intake and was fine for the rest of the trip.

It's RACE DAY Again

Race day number 2 had arrived. I was in my Minnie Mouse "costume" and Jennifer in her Cinderella "costume." (Obviously, they were adapted for running, not like actual Halloween costumes). Stephanie was running on her own and went ahead of us. Unfortunately, I quickly realized I had forgotten my headphones in the room. This was a little scary as 13.1 miles is a long way to go without my music.

We stopped for a few pictures including the awesome pic in front of Cinderella Castle. If you ever do a runDisney race that goes through Magic Kingdom, I suggest you plan for that pic- it's such an epic spot and keepsake to have. How many people get the opportunity to see Cinderella Castle? How many people get the opportunity to run through that castle? It's one of my favorite pics!

Anyway, we were cruising along. I was rambling incessantly due to my lack of headphones and therefore no distraction of music. It was getting hot quickly, but we kept plugging away. I'm pretty sure I was driving Jennifer crazy with my constant chatter because she kept telling me I could go on ahead if I wanted to. I didn't. I couldn't. God wanted me to stay with her, and that was what I was going to do. I was totally ok with it and just trying to enjoy the experience. All the Disney stuff, the scenery, the bands, the people cheering, the golf course, the resorts, all the music and of course Disney magic.

Eventually, with another round of, "You can go on ahead if you want," I said, "Ok, but not until we get you over the hills." I knew that some tough inclines were coming up in the last few miles. I knew this because I learned of them the hard way when I ran this course in 2014. You remember my description from the half in 2014? This was the same course as that one.

She was ok with that. I think that once we got to those hills, she was grateful I had stayed with her. Although I had warned her about them, I think they are worse when you have them staring you in the face, and you have no choice but to go up them. We made it up all of them and then had about 2 miles to go before the finish.

She was more than happy to let me stay with her the rest of the way. I'm so glad she was. That time we had on that course is priceless to me! I will never forget it! If you ever have the opportunity to run a race with someone and be their buddy to help them conquer it, please do! That is an incredible gift. I cherish that every time I get the opportunity to do so.

We started and finished that race together. Every single step of those 13.1 miles we covered together. Jennifer was now officially a half-marathoner! We received our awesome medals. I also received my super fantastic challenge medal. My first official runDisney challenge was complete! Such great memories, but boy was it exhausting!

Chapter Sixteen

Coast-to-Coast

So, with that challenge now behind us.. what would happen to the dream of the pink Coast-to-Coast medals? We still didn't know. Steph and I still wanted to do it but didn't know how to make it happen. And I say Steph and I, but really, I mean me. She was happy to come along for the ride with me but was still so new to this Disney thing that she just humored me in participating in all my constant Disneyness!

She does love to run though and knew enough runners that respect and love runDisney races that many of them have them on their "bucket list." So, she was excited about the opportunity if we could find a way to make it happen. Was it going to be super disappointing to her if it didn't work out? No, probably not. The only thing was, she didn't want to see me disappointed if it didn't. We kept it in God's hands and knew without a doubt that if He wanted us to go, He would, again, make it clear that was what He wanted.

Suddenly, little pieces started falling into place that were making it clear that this was becoming a pretty good possibility. I happened to be off work the weekend of the races. David, who is the master of rewards points, by the way, had rewards points for the room that he let us use as well as airline miles to use for our flights. Now, all we had to do was pay for our race registrations and our park tickets. My in-laws had two unused gift passes that they offered up to me as a thank you. Now, we were just down to tickets for Kenzie and Steph. Ok, let's do this! God gave us enough signals that we knew now He wanted to fulfill this dream that had been created a year and a half earlier.

Looking back, I'm still incredibly thankful for this and the way it worked out. I absolutely could have been stressing and fretting and trying to make this happen on my own. But that's not how this running thing is supposed to be. God gave it to me, and I only want to run what He wants me to run. This is His story and His plan, not mine! Sure, I had the idea in my head I wanted to do it, but that didn't mean that it was a good idea for me or part of God's plan. I just sat back and patiently waited for Him to show us one way or the other. And, He did!

Disneyland Planning

None of us had ever been to Disneyland at this point, so I was continually trying to learn everything I could about it. You probably think, well it's Disney, aren't they the same? Nope, not by a long shot. So many things are different out there compared to the one in Florida. One of the most noticeable differences is the size. Here's a fun fact. You could fit the entire Disneyland Resort in the parking lot of Magic Kingdom in Florida! Imagine that!

Disneyland was the original park that Walt Disney himself created. That alone was going to make it super fantastic. That was where it all started. Being the Disney fan that I am, I was super excited to get to experience that.

We chose to do the challenge again, similar to the Princess weekend. The schedule was the same: 10K on Saturday and half marathon on Sunday. One of the super fun aspects of this race weekend is that it falls over Mother's Day weekend. What an excellent way to spend my Mother's Day!

By the time it was clear that this was a go, the challenge was once again sold out. Thankfully, the travel agent that we had gotten Steph's Princess bib from still had some spots left. So, we signed up through her and were all set.

Given that Disneyland is so much smaller, and we were trying to keep this trip to the bare minimum in terms of money, it was a very short trip. We flew out early Friday morning and were returning late Monday night.

In my research, I had found some "must do's" that I wanted us to partake in. One was the 24-layer chocolate cake. Yes, 24 layers of chocolate cake. It was FANTASTIC! We were smart enough to share one piece between the 3 of us, and oh it was so worth it!

One of the super exciting things at Disneyland is to experience some of the same attractions we love at Disney World and see how they differ and compare. There are quite a few. There are also plenty of attractions that are not in Florida, so those were fun to experience as well.

I do not like heights, and yet they made me go on Mickey's Fun Wheel. This is a giant Ferris wheel. I do not like the small versions of these at carnivals, so I'm pretty sure I went kicking and screaming. We quickly realized they had spinning cars and not spinning cars. I insisted that if they were going to drag me on it, we were NOT riding in a spinning car! No way, no how. It was our turn to load, and we were blessed to get to ride with an amazing 90-year-old grandma and one of her grandsons. It was her birthday, and he brought her to Disneyland. She had spent every single birthday at Disneyland since it opened. What a special gift! It was a great distraction for me as she was more than happy to talk about all this, which allowed me to stay focused entirely on her and the conversation and totally miss the fact that we were like 900 miles in the air on this crazy wheel! We finally made it back to the bottom, and I survived. Check that off the list!

We also got to ride California Screamin'. Kenzie and I rode in the front row, because well... if you're going to ride on it, that's exactly what you do. That ride was amazing! I was sure the car was going to fall off the track because of the view and the feel that you get when sitting in the front row. It was so thrilling! The front row was definitely an excellent choice for that ride. If you aren't much of a roller coaster person, I would suggest going further back. It seemed much less intense back there when we rode it again. Since our time there, the ride has experienced a makeover and a new theme and therefore a new name, "The Incredicoaster." I'm confident it will still be a fantastic ride, and I hope that I can make it back out there to experience the new version.

Let's get back to the races. In my massive amounts of research, it became apparent that due to some wording in the runDisney information, we would not only earn the super awesome pink Coast-to-Coast medal, but we would also earn the normal blue one. This was over-the-top exciting to me. I'm a medal girl! You are probably starting to pick up on this! I love the bling! And now we were going to earn five new medals this weekend.

We, of course, brought our Princess medals with us so that we could eventually get pictures with all eight medals once we had completed the challenge. I bet you are sitting there like really? Yes, really! And we weren't the only ones. I researched and asked in Facebook groups (because again that's where you are supposed to get all your great information, right?), and this is a very common and reasonable thing to do... at least for Disney runners anyway.

Chapter Seventeen

It's RACE DAY

It didn't take us long to realize it was pouring rain while we were getting ready for the 10K. We were hoping it would stop before we had to walk to the corrals, but if not, what was our plan? It wasn't cold, so that wasn't so bad. We both had hats/visors already planned to keep rain out of our eyes, but it would be a lot nicer not to get completely drenched before we even started. We had not prepared for the rain. I always bring ponchos to Florida with us, and for whatever reason, those didn't seem necessary on our journey to California. However, as we were discussing options, I remembered reading a tip from other runners on Facebook. Grab a garbage bag from the hotel, not the small ones, but the ones they use for their carts.

Well, what did we have to lose? We found an employee willing to give us a couple of garbage bags to use as makeshift ponchos. We made some holes for our heads and off we went. They worked out great as a nice throw-away poncho. Thankfully, it did stop raining before the race started, and therefore we were able to lose our garbage bags quickly. After all, we had awesome costumes underneath that we wanted people to see. Plus, running in a garbage bag is not ideal... Doable but not ideal.

One of the huge differences between races at Disney World versus Disneyland is the walk to the corrals. We could walk from our hotel (you cannot do this at all in Florida) to the corrals. And that walk was a much shorter walk than in Florida from where the buses drop you off to where you go to get to the corrals. That was a welcome perk. It especially comes into play after the race. You don't have to wait for transportation, and you don't have to wait for the transportation to get you to your resort. You can leave when you are done and walk back, provided your hotel is close enough.

Steph was in corral A, and I was B. We had decided again that we would not run together, and she would start from her corral rather than back in mine. This was fine with me. She is faster than me, and I didn't want to slow her down or make her feel like she had to go slow for me. We parted ways to go to our designated corrals and waited for the start.

This was a super fun course. I felt as though we spent quite a bit of time in the parks. Given I hadn't been to either of these parks ever, it was super awesome as everything was new and exciting. I felt good running, maybe a little too good. As my phone kept updating me on my pace, I kept telling myself that I was going way too fast. I mean, it wasn't too fast for this race, it was too fast given that I still had the half the next day. I was worried that I wouldn't have anything left for that race, and I had hoped for a good time on the half. I kept trying to slow down, but just couldn't. It felt good, so I just kept running. I was concerned I would eventually see the aftermath of this the next day because as much as I tried, I couldn't slow down enough for what I thought I should be doing. I finished with a respectable time, and we were off to clean up and get ready for an adventure in the parks.

It's RACE DAY #2 God's Race, God's Pace

It's time for the half marathon. Remember my goal of a PR back in the Disney World half that God had a different idea about? I had brought this idea back. I figured since God was making this race happen, that maybe He wanted me to PR at it too. My dream goal was to finish with a time of 2 hours and 15 minutes or less. Although this was my goal, I didn't think I had a realistic chance of accomplishing it since it involved back to back races. But, there's nothing wrong with setting goals, right? I was pretty sure that if I were running the half alone, that was a reasonable expectation. However, with the 10K the day before, I didn't think it would be possible.

Don't forget that we had been adventuring around the theme parks the entire day after the 10K. There was no time to rest. We couldn't waste time sleeping. There was so much to see and do.

Days before the race I felt "nudged" to try to find and run with the 2:15 pacer during the race. For those who don't know, a pacer is someone that runs a specific pace the entire race to ensure that you finish in that amount of time. Since it was a "nudge" you know by now I had to listen because those nudges are God telling me that's what He wants.

I was successful in my attempt to find her before the race in our corral. The pacer held a sign that had balloons attached to it and that said the desired finish time, in this case, 2:15. This would make it easy to spot on the course. There were over 13,000 runners so keeping track of 1 runner would've been challenging to say the least without that visual.

She told us we would be maintaining a 10 minute per mile pace throughout and walk through the water stations. I hadn't put any actual math to my goal time because my internal reaction to this information was like "What? There is NO way I can keep up a 10-minute pace for 13 miles. Shorter distances yes, but not for a full 13 miles!" Well apparently, that's what needs to happen if you are going to accomplish a 2:15 half. My suggestion - if you set a goal finish time, maybe do the math ahead of time, so you know what you are trying to do. This way, you don't have sticker shock, so to speak, as I did.

I figured, well I'm here, I guess I might as well try and stick with her as long as I can. I started with her and the other women trying to accomplish the same goal. However, I lost them before we even reached mile 1. Yep, I didn't even make it a mile. There were two big hills in the beginning and quite a few people to maneuver through that I just couldn't make it happen. I was back on my own which didn't bother me too badly as this is how I run all the time. However, it was a jolt to my head as I was sure that was what God wanted me to do, and I wasn't even able to stick with her a mile. We had barely started the race, and I already felt like I had let Him down.

Shortly after this, I started experiencing some significant technical difficulties. I use my "smartphone" to play music through my headphones (thankfully I remembered the headphones this time!) as well as to keep track of my miles, pacing, etc. My music started skipping and was just totally messed up. As I was fumbling with my phone trying to get it working, I was confident that all these distractions were causing me to slow down tremendously.

I even thought about stopping to see if I could fix it, but I didn't want to stop. I was frustrated as I was counting on the lyrics to keep me going and keep me focused on why and for whom I was running. Eventually, the music started working, but I didn't realize that the app that tells me my pace and distance (I had it set to update me every half mile) had stopped working in the process. It was still tracking me, but it wasn't going to tell me anything. I felt as though I was running blind. I guess I had become quite dependent on these stats.

Needless to say, this was all incredibly frustrating. I was again certain this was where God wanted me to be and what He wanted me to be doing, but I couldn't understand why all this stuff was messing up and not working the way I thought it should. How was I going to get this PR if I was fumbling with all these technical difficulties and messing with all these distractions?

Thankfully, I was able to put my focus back on what I was doing and why I was there. God wanted me there! God put me there! God wanted me doing this race! It was His race, and I needed to give it back to Him! As I let go and just gave control of all of it back to Him, I calmed down, and the frustrations left.

Through all this, there were signs with the same phrase that I kept seeing. The phrase just really spoke to me "Just keep running." (Yes, it's a reference to the movie *Finding Dory* when Dory says "just keep swimming") That's exactly what I needed to do and exactly what I did.

There were obviously mile markers on the course, so I did at least know where I was. They had timers at each, so I had a rough guess (very rough!) of my time. I love math but have never been good at doing it in my head and certainly am not capable of computing things in my head while running! That is WAY out of my league!

Around mile 8 or 9 I spotted a pacing sign way up ahead with balloons. I was shocked, to say the least! I was so shocked that for a minute I thought maybe it was the 2:30 pacer (meaning I was going much slower than I had hoped). As I got closer, I could tell it was the 2:15 pacer because I recognized her clothing. I was like "WHAT? HOW IS THIS POSSIBLE? How am I catching up to them?"

I did catch up to them and ran with them for a couple of miles. The pacer told us at about mile 11 that we were ahead of the pace by about a minute and would likely finish at 2:14! Again, "WHAT?!" That almost stopped me in my tracks! There is no way! How could this be? I turned my focus back to what/who had gotten me to this point... I kept praying for God to be in control and that I run the race He wanted me to run and kept telling myself "just keep running, just keep running."

From then on, my goal was making sure that I didn't let the pacer get close enough that there was a threat that they may pass me. The last mile or so I couldn't even hear them anymore. I knew they weren't that far back there, but at least I had enough of a buffer that I couldn't hear them. As I was getting closer to the finish line and realized I was going to beat my goal time of 2:15, I realized that it was all part of His plan.

All the frustrations and struggles at the beginning of the race needed to happen. Had it all worked as I thought/expected it to, I would have run the entire race, but I would've been running much more slowly. My app would've been telling me what my pace was, and I would've convinced myself that I couldn't keep that pace up for 13 miles. I would have said to myself that I needed to slow down if I wanted to be able to keep running the whole race.

I was wrong! God knew what I was capable of and by taking away those stats, I had to trust Him and "just keep running." If I hadn't had the nudge in the beginning to find the pacer, I would never have known what to look for once I lost her. So, even the not keeping up with her was part of the plan. Seeing the pacer up ahead and knowing I still had a shot at the PR was a huge turning point in the race for me. The result of all of this was that I was capable of so much more than I ever could've imagined! My official finishing time was 2:14:03!

Fun fact - this is the only finishing time to this day that I can remember the exact time. All the rest I can give you a pretty good idea like my first half was a 2:30 something. This is the only one I can give you exactly at any given moment.

I had tears when I crossed that finish line. Happy tears of course! I could not believe I had done it. Tears continued when they gave me the medals. I finally found Steph, and I'm not even sure she could understand me as I was ugly crying while trying to tell her this fantastic story of my PR. I'm so thankful she was there. I can't imagine that journey without her. This will forever be in my heart.

This was one of the significant turning points for me in this journey. I finally figured out that so much of running is like life. Those "struggles" I was experiencing were symbolic of struggles in everyday life. As I gave God back the control over ALL of it, His plan for me was able to become a reality.

I don't pretend that my race "struggles" come anywhere close to some of life's struggles, but the point is no matter how tough your battle or situation is, He is in control. If you surrender it all to Him, He will guide you through it. That is a promise He has made to us! I also don't pretend that life's struggles can be solved in 2 hours. In fact, sometimes this can take many years, but the result is still that He is there with us every step of the way, and His plan will prevail! We can take great comfort in that!

I need to share another fantastic point in this race. I knew ahead of time that the Red Hat Society Ladies were there. Again, all my Facebook research had given me a clue to watch out for them. I had no idea the impact they would have. If you aren't familiar with them, I'm sure there is a local group of them in your area. They are a group of ladies that get together to have fun. You will recognize them by their distinctly obvious red hats. I remember getting ready to turn a corner onto another street at maybe mile 7 or 8. I was hearing a lot of music, cheering, and clapping and was anxiously awaiting getting there to see what wonderful things were up ahead. As I turned that corner, I could see them. I had found the Red Hat Society Ladies. They were awesome. They were all so happy for us. They cheered. They danced. They clapped. They high-fived. There were so many of them. Once I thought I had indeed come to the end of them, there were more. It seemed like they covered almost the entire block. If they didn't, it was super close.

If I remember correctly, I think I read there were something like 700 of them! It was such an amazing and inspirational site. Think about it - they came from all over the country to come and cheer us on. That is incredible! They were so fun. I don't think there was a dry eye for any of us runners as we passed them. I don't know how it could not make you a little emotional. It was a beautiful experience. Unfortunately, however, they weren't able to come back in 2017.

Sadly, now the Disneyland races are on what is hopefully only a temporary hiatus. There is a large amount of construction and refurbishments going on out there preparing for some super awesome additions to the already amazing parks and resort areas. I am hoping that once these projects are completed, we will see the races come back as they really were fun! So, at this point, this was one of the last times the pink Coast-to-Coast Challenge was even a possibility as 2017 was the last year for the Tinker Bell race weekend.

Chapter Eighteen

Costumes

L et's talk costumes for a little bit. Yes, running in a costume is a real thing, especially at Disney. Some runners will go to great lengths and creativity for their costumes, others take a more casual approach. One thing is for sure at Disney races pretty much anything goes in terms of costumes as long as you stay within the guidelines Disney has in place.

When we were preparing for the Princess races, there was a lot of time spent trying to determine the "perfect" costumes. Do you match, do you have a theme, is it going to be hot/cold? Jennifer quickly chose a Cinderella costume that she purchased as a set online. I had picked Minnie for the half marathon because, well it's Minnie. She seems like the original princess to me.

I am not the most creative person, so I needed a simple costume to create. I made a red tutu for my Minnie costume and used some white felt cut into circles that I hot glued onto the tutu. Yes, this does work. We attached a yellow bow to the front and, and it was done. That was the start of it anyway.

I needed to make this first and quickly because I wanted to send it with my in-laws when they left for the winter. I was worried about how ruined it would get when I shoved it into my luggage. They generously transported it down there for me and kept it safe and poofy until we got there.

I already had a black running tank top and some black shorts for underneath the tutu. I also made some shoe covers out of yellow felt to have Minnie shoes. I secured them to my shoes by making holes for the laces and just laced the shoes normally. They were perfect. I never even knew they were there.

We still needed an idea for the 10K. Kenzie and I were visiting my sister Bobbie for a weekend and while in Walmart, we glanced through the fabric section. There was a scrap bin that we decided to thumb through to see if we could get any inspiration from any of the pieces.

Sure enough, there was a sheer fabric with sparkly snowflakes on it. It was beautiful. Keep in mind this was about the time the movie *Frozen* was very popular, and the new ride was even in the works at Epcot. We thought it would make a perfect cape for an Elsa costume. That marked the beginning of our matching Elsa costumes.

We eventually found some shiny, blue fabric to use for our Elsa skirts. Neither Kenzie nor I are super gifted in sewing. However, we can hold our own with basic tasks on the sewing machine. We didn't do anything fancy just a hem and the two seams at the top with some elastic running through it. We decided it still needed something though. We found some snowflakes in the Christmas decorations that we glued to the skirts for more effect.

We were able to find some blue tank tops that matched pretty well. Kenzie drew and cut out snowflakes out of shiny silver fabric. We attached them to the front of the tank tops, and we made short capes out of the sheer fabric and attached those to the shoulders of the tank tops. They were adorable if I do say so myself. We did have to add a partial tutu underneath the skirts to give them a little bit of poof. For a 10K they didn't seem like they would be too bad to try and run in.

We convinced Steph to try and dress up too. Remember this was her first experience with runDisney races, and the whole idea of a costume while she was racing was foreign to her. Tinker Bell is her favorite character, so she had a small green tutu for one of the races, and she had a Snow White themed tutu for the other because it matched her shoes and socks. They were super cute outfits! However, she vowed never to wear a tutu during a race again. I didn't have any significant issues with my costume choices, and thankfully the weather was decent that we didn't have to add layers to stay warm.

For the Tinker Bell weekend, I wanted to keep the expenses down, so I didn't want to go extreme on costumes. I also didn't have a lot of time to put into creating one. I decided that I needed to wear my 2 "church shirts" (The race shirts with our church logo on the front and the bible verse on the back). One was blue, and the other was pink. (They were the same shirt just different colors. I had had a pink one made for the half in 2014.) The next step was trying to get creative and come up with something that could be created using those, and with hopefully some things we already had at home.

Ashley was a fan of the Cheshire Cat and had gotten a Cheshire Cat visor one year while we were at Disney World. The real perk was that actually I knew where that was. My running shoes were pink, so they already matched. Kenzie had a pink tutu from one of her Homecoming costumes. All I needed at that point to complete this was some purple tulle (the poofy fabric used to make tutus) to make stripes with the pink for the tutu, and I would be all set. That was going to be my costume for the half.

For the 10K, I was working with the blue shirt. I still had the yellow shoe covers from Minnie, and I had a blue visor. We decided this would be perfect for Donald Duck. We made a white tutu and added a black tie to the visor like Donald's hat, and there we had it. I don't think I spent more than $10 to put these together, so it was definitely a win.

Unfortunately, these weren't quite as comfortable as the first two costumes. Or, it may have been because I was running faster and working much harder in these races than I did with the others, but I had decided after the half marathon that the tutus were a no go for me now as well. The tulle was causing chafing on my legs, and nobody needs any more chafing than what you naturally get during a race. But, I will say the costumes were ADORABLE!

Chapter Nineteen

Becoming a travel agent

After we did the two big race weekends at the respective Disney resorts, with me doing the bulk of all the planning, Steph and David were encouraging me to pursue the idea of becoming a travel agent that specializes in Disney. The rest of my family had been telling me this for years.

I was always in charge of making all our resort reservations and making sure all the planning details were taken care of. They all just let me take over. I'm not sure if it was because they knew I loved it, or if they just preferred not to have to do it themselves. Either way, they were right. I did love it. I didn't know anything about becoming a travel agent. I did, however, know how to plan a multi family Disney trip, and I knew about runDisney race weekends.

Since we had already purchased bibs from a travel agent, we found on the runDisney website, this seemed like a logical place to start. There is a list of agencies that offer travel packages for race weekends. I started with this list of agencies. I researched them the best I could from their websites and other internet finds.

I was quickly drawn to one and contacted the owner. One of my favorite tasks during that process was creating my "Disney resume." How many people can say they have a "Disney resume?" This consisted of all things relevant to and representative of my knowledge of Disney planning. It included all the trips we had taken to that point, the variety of different resorts that we had stayed in, the various parks we visited, events we experienced, the races, my daughters' dance competitions, and more. I have to say; it was super fun to put that together. It allowed me to see how this whole thing had really come together. Each trip and every detail of those trips that helped me develop not just my knowledge but my deep love for Disney and the planning involved in a Disney vacation.

After a lengthy and challenging recruiting process, I was chosen to join the wonderful Wish Upon a Star with Us family. Again, how could this be? Was God really letting this happen? Was this really His plan for me? Yes! This was and is a dream come true. God was ready for this to be part of my journey. If you know me at all, you know of my love for Disney and my love of running. Now, I get to do them both for God! How incredible is that? Again, thank you God for putting each and every piece of this plan together in Your way and Your timing!

Chapter Twenty

"Grace Wins"

I really hadn't had any intention of ever considering doing a marathon until about June or July. Since I had consistently been keeping my distance up due to the challenges and then training for the St. Jude run, this seemed like the logical next step. However, before this point, I kept saying, "Running for 5 or 6 hours at one time for a marathon is not something I ever want to do." Clearly, that idea didn't take long to change.

There was a marathon in Peoria in October that I had considered doing. However, I had injured my foot during the St. Jude run. Once it didn't heal within a matter of a few days, I knew that it was absolutely my clue that I wasn't supposed to run that race.

For me to have been able to run the marathon, I would have needed to continue with a VERY consistent training plan and long distances. The injury had me not running at all, so I knew I wouldn't be able to just pick back up where I left off. I knew that marathon was not what God wanted me to run, so I was totally ok with not running and letting the foot heal. I knew He would let me know when He was ready for me to run again.

Is this starting to sound familiar? It should. This is a very similar situation to what happened 3 years prior when I thought maybe it was time to run a half.

I didn't run for a month after the St. Jude Run. We had plans on a Saturday morning and that Friday night before when I was getting ready to head for bed, I felt this unmistakable "nudge". It was telling me to get my running clothes out and go for a run in the morning. I was waiting for God to let me know when He wanted me to run again, and He just told me it was time! I obeyed and ran a couple miles the next morning with relative ease. I was able to continue to run symptom-free and started on a 3 runs per week plan again. I started with shorter distances though because I didn't have any plans for a race in the near future.

Shortly after getting back to running I was feeling some nudges about the marathon at Disney World. The nudges kept coming, but I kept not believing them. After all, He had already let me run my first half marathon at Disney World. I absolutely didn't deserve to be given that same gift for my first marathon. I know that's not how God works but it's still what I was feeling. I really struggled with not deserving this. However, the nudges kept coming, and I continued to question them.

I asked Him for just 1 more sign that I couldn't possibly ignore or question. I know this too is not how this is supposed to work, but I asked anyway. This was a Friday, and the deadline for submitting a proof time for the marathon was in a couple days, so I knew if it was going to happen, I needed to decide fast.

Remember when this whole thing started and there was a client at work that mentioned the races at Disney? The one that prompted the first race we did at Disney? Well, guess who was scheduled that day? Yep, her! I was chatting with her, and as I was talking to her, it was all coming back. I remember thinking, "Wow God that's a pretty amazing sign, but is it really a sign?" I know I know, but sometimes I'm a slow learner.

I had planned to go for a short 3-mile run on my lunch break. She was our last patient before the break. I don't always run on my lunch, but sometimes it just works out well. On that run, I was trying to comprehend all of this and determine if this was in fact what God wanted me to do. The very last song that played before I finished the run was "Grace Wins" by Matthew West. That was God saying to me, "I know that you mess up, but running is what I want you to do for me, and I want you to run THIS race for me!" I remember thinking, "Ok God, you can't make it much clearer than that! I'm in"

I signed up that day! Even though I knew this was what I was supposed to do and was excited, I was also terrified of this 26.2-mile journey.

Steph and I had been chatting about this, and she agreed that she would run it too if it turned out I was going to. When we knew it was what I was supposed to do, she was all in too. So, the planning and training were officially going to begin.

Chapter Twenty-One

Bobbie

My youngest sister, Bobbie, was also a significant part of this journey. She had been a great listener, a mentor, and offered me counsel on hundreds of occasions over the years. She consistently helped me to stay focused on God and to learn what He was telling me.

She had listened to Christian audiobooks for years and was encouraging me to read or listen to some books since she had learned so much by doing this herself. I resisted because I'm not a reader. It tends to put me to sleep.

I listened to a Christian radio station on my phone a lot while working around the house. I kept telling her no, it wasn't for me. I didn't think I could get things done the same if I was listening to a book versus the music. And, the music had been VITAL to my journey.

I don't remember exactly how it came about, but I finally agreed to try one of the books. It was likely a God nudge. She started me on a series of books. I don't remember the titles, but they were primarily about walking angels and how they come into the characters' lives to help fulfill God's purpose and plan. People that kept them on the path He wanted for them, not the path they were headed in. The angels were just regular people that saved the characters from getting hit by a car, meeting the wrong person, taking the wrong job, other things that would cause them to be deterred from God's path for their life.

After one book I was hooked. These books kept me in a zone. I was hearing about all these wonderful God miracles in these people's lives. Yes, these were fictional books, but clearly, this is something very real in our world. I had never thought about it like this though. I quickly went through these books.

I'm not sure how many books I went through that fall, but it was a lot. I didn't listen to them while I was running. I stayed with my Christian music. I'm just not sure how listening to a book while running would work for me, but I guess it's something I could try. But, I listened to them while I did everything else. I cleaned, worked, got ready, did dishes, and cooked, all while listening to these books. They were quite addictive, but clearly in a good way. I finally understood why Bobbie was always listening to them.

The walking angels series was probably my favorite. They demonstrated some of the fantastic ways God always steps in to help us. We don't even realize it most of the time, but man, He has some amazing resources that he uses. I couldn't think of a walking angel that had come into my life like in these books, but I was sure there had been some. I'm confident we all have them. How wonderful is that? God loves us so much that He sends angels to help make sure we continue down His path. And, they step in just at the perfect moments.

If you are looking for a different way to experience God, I would highly recommend some Christian audiobooks. I have since gotten out of this routine, but maybe someday it will become my "thing" again. This was a fantastic way to keep me focused on God and this marathon journey He had me on. I needed to stay focused to run the race for Him, after all, He was the one giving me the opportunity to do the race and wanted me in it for a reason.

Chapter Twenty-Two

It's RACE DAY

I went into this race expecting it to be much harder than anything I had ever done. It proved to be that and then some, even more than I could've imagined. I was cruising along and doing fabulously. I was enjoying all the sights, Cinderella Castle at Magic Kingdom, the bands, the DJ's, then Animal Kingdom, more fun on the open road, I was truly in my happy place until about mile 17 or 18. I had some aches and pains prior to that, but they weren't significant enough that they were hindering my mojo.

If you have had any experience with runners, you have probably heard them refer to something known as "hitting the wall." Unless you are a runner, you likely don't know what this means. I hit the wall and hit it hard! This happened for me near the Wide World of Sports Complex part of the course, around the 18-mile mark. In an instant I went from telling myself, "You can do this ½ mile at a time." And "You only have 8 miles left, 7 miles left, etc. It will be tough, but you can run 7 miles easily just take it 1/2 mile at a time" to "I can't run another half mile! How am I going to finish this? I need to walk; I don't want to walk, if I walk I won't be able to run anymore, I need to stop." It was horrible!

I had come so far but just felt as though I had nothing left. I hadn't trained for intervals, and usually, when I stop running, I can't start back up again. I was scared, super scared. I was exhausted. My knee was feeling like it wanted to give out and was hurting. I knew it wasn't capable of running 7 or 8 more miles. My shoulders were on fire, but I had convinced myself they weren't an issue as I didn't need them to run. However, I couldn't say the same thing about my knee. It is essential in trying to run. I knew it wasn't my knee, but instead, my hamstring, which was overworked and just plain over this race.

I did have to start walking. I stopped at a medical tent to rub some Biofreeze on my knee as that was the only area I could access with my pants on. I didn't even think about rubbing it over the pants. Lesson learned for next time. From here I started a run for a bit, walk for a bit strategy, otherwise known as intervals. However, I didn't have a set time for each interval, so I was winging it.

I was on a walk break and happened to look ahead of me just about the time I was going to start running again. That's when I saw it, the mountain in front of me. It was just an on-ramp, but a very steep one, and at mile 21, that was a mountain. There was no way anyone was going to convince me otherwise! I can't imagine what my body language was saying exactly. Apparently, from the back of me, it was undeniable how devastating and defeating this moment was because at that exact moment, another runner that was apparently right behind me was now right beside me saying, "I think we both just had the same reaction to seeing that at the same time."

I'll be honest; I was crying. Crying over the 4+ hours I had put in knowing I still had over an hour to go, especially if I was going to walk. Crying over being exhausted. Crying at the pain that came and went and came back in my knee. Crying at the fact that I wanted to quit. Crying at the mountain that lurked ahead! We decided we would climb the mountain together!

At about the middle of this "mountain" was a Green Army Guy from the movie *Toy Story*. He was yelling at runners to hurry up, to do push-ups and all sorts of other comments that I feared. He was yelling at them, and although it was meant to be fun and inspirational, at that point, I was terrified. I was worried he was going to yell at me, which would cause me to burst into more tears. I was worried he would single me out, and I wasn't going to be able to respond to whatever he yelled at me to do. I was worried I would give up if he yelled at me. This was the opposite of his intent, but the fear allowed all of those thoughts and the "what if's" to fill my mind. God was protecting me and knew that I couldn't have handled him choosing me to yell at, so we just walked on past him.

I didn't realize it until after the race, but remember those books on the walking angels? This was my walking angel sent from God to keep me going and not give up. His name was Ryan, and he was from Raleigh, North Carolina. He was a young gentleman (I searched for him in the race results to make sure he had finished and found out he was 26). Poor guy was in shorts and a tank top. He had to have been freezing as the temperature was only in the 30s when we started the race.

I honestly don't have any idea how long he had been behind me or where he came from. All I remember was my complete and utter feeling of defeat when I saw that "mountain." My head dropped, and my heart sank. At that very moment was when he started talking. I don't want to think about what might have happened had this fellow runner not appeared at that exact moment. I'm honestly not sure I would have finished the race.

We managed to get through the next couple of miles chatting, and the distraction kept both of us from pursuing the idea of not finishing. We didn't talk about all sorts of positive things. In fact, it was quite the opposite. We were whining and complaining about how horrible of an idea this was and what on Earth were we doing here. This seems to be normal in this state of exhaustion I think because this hits me on quite a few runs. We discussed his running history. He had run some 5Ks and 10Ks but nothing like a marathon. I had to ask how he decided to do a marathon.

He said he had been at Disney World the year before when the race was going on. He had been at Hollywood Studios and saw the runners coming through that park. He thought they all looked like they were having a great deal of fun and an excellent time. He wanted to try it. He wanted to see what all this fun was about, so he signed up. However, he had changed his mind at this point. He said that when we got to Hollywood Studios, we should make sure we don't look happy and like we're having a good time. He didn't want to give another innocent bystander the same wrong impression he had gotten the year before.

I'm literally laughing out loud as I'm typing this. If you could hear the things we speak and think on a race course, you would probably wonder why we ever do this if it's so horrible. Well, we ask ourselves that a lot at these moments. It's the finish that changes it all!

Anyway, we made the pact not to be smiling and misleading anyone. He couldn't run at all due to his leg muscles. His quads had had enough of running, and he was stuck walking the rest of the way.

Once we finally arrived at Hollywood Studios, I knew we had 3 miles to go, and it was all within Disney areas that would be filled with spectators, families, signs, volunteers, and random park goers. I decided then that I wasn't done running, and I was going to try and run that last 3 miles to try and finish strong. I told him that I needed to try and run as much of the rest as I could. I knew that God didn't put me out there and give me that race to run to give up. I felt bad leaving him, but I had to try. I had to do it for God. Ryan said he would keep an eye on me as I ran ahead in case I stopped and had to walk. If so, he would try to catch back up to me if he could.

We parted ways and off I went on my way back to solo running. It certainly wasn't an easy 3 miles like I'm used to. By the time I finally made it to Epcot and the World Showcase I was hobbling badly, but I wasn't going to stop. I was familiar with the end of this course as it was the same finish as the half marathon. I remembered that there was a little area that was hidden from any spectators or really anyone other than other runners. My knee was buckling badly, and my hobbling version of jogging had gotten worse. I thought that if I gave it a tiny break, it would let me finish running strong. I made it to that area and gave it a small walk break. That was all I needed. I started back to a run and then I could see it. The finish line was within sight and getting closer!

I kept putting one foot in front of the other and keeping the pace until finally... I did it! I crossed the finish line and completed my first marathon. I was officially a marathoner! Wow! I still have a hard time believing this is my reality!

I had been cruising along at a comfortable 11 minute per mile pace, which I would've been excited about for a finish time. However, once I hit the wall, pace was quickly gone. But, here's the fun part! Remember that first Steamboat Race back in 2011 when this whole journey started? I was ecstatic that I finished that race with an 11:58 per mile pace.

Do you want to know what my pace was (based on my app) for this race? A MARATHON! 26.2 miles! 11:58 per mile! I naturally had assumed I would be a little faster than that, but my first and most important goal was to finish. I finished, and I finished 26.2 miles at the exact same pace that 6-1/2 years prior I could barely do 4 miles in! CRAZY! Once again God's race, God's pace!

I did try to find Ryan on Facebook and in Facebook groups, but I never did. I just wanted to thank him for being my walking angel that day. I genuinely don't know what would've happened if God hadn't placed him there at that exact spot. I was seriously ready to give up and quit. But thankfully, God had a better plan. He stepped in and gave me exactly what I needed to switch gears in my body and my brain and to be able to finish strong.

Ryan if you happen to read this book, THANK YOU! You may never know how important those 2 miles were in the grand scheme of my life, but I do. They were life changing for sure. I went from possibly becoming a marathon quitter to a marathon finisher! Thank you, Jesus!

Chapter Twenty-Three

Funny Story

Here's a funny side story to all of this. Remember that app that my family was able to track me with the last time? We had set up the same thing, but with a new app so pretty much everyone could track Stephanie and I. The plan was for David and Kenzie to meet us at the finishing area. Everyone else was cheering us on, but we would actually meet up with them after we had time to shower and clean up a little back in the rooms.

It was very cold that day. My phone had issues with the battery dying in the cold really fast. I knew ahead of time it was going to be cold, so I planned ahead. I had brought some extra socks that were thick. I stored my phone in the sock in the water pouch of my running belt. As long as I didn't take it out and look at it, which is difficult while you are running anyway, I was hopeful that it would make it to the end.

David and Kenzie were watching the tracking and of course, Steph was done way before me. Once I hit the finish line, I took my phone out to stop the running app. As soon as I did that my phone instantly died and wouldn't turn back on.

Of course, I was crying. Yes, again. I was crying because I had finished. I was crying because I was exhausted. I was crying because I was in pain with my knee. Crying because of the people congratulating us at the medal area. Crying at everything. I made my way through all of that slowly and on to where they give you the famous runDisney snack box and banana.

I hobbled my way through trying to get to the other side to find my people. I had no phone to try and call them or text them, so this was going to be interesting. Thousands of people and I was going to try and find my people. I made it to the other side and looked around some with no luck.

I found a woman and asked if I could use her phone to try and find them. She, of course, said yes, but I was so out of it I didn't think I could dial the phone. I asked her to dial for me. I was able to remember Kenzie's number, but as it was ringing, I thought to myself, "she isn't going to answer because she doesn't recognize the number." Sure enough, she didn't. I then asked her to dial David's number. He always answers his phone. Nope, not this time. He didn't answer again because he didn't recognize the number either. (And apparently, they didn't notice it was the same number.) Unfortunately, she then had to go meet up with some of her people and couldn't help me any longer. I continued to wander around aimlessly for a little bit. I was trying to find another nice person to ask to borrow their phone. Any person I saw probably would've said yes, but in my half delusional state I was too scared to ask.

I don't know how much time passed, but I did find someone else to ask to borrow their phone. She naturally said yes, and at this point, I felt comfortable dialing myself. I tried David again just hoping he would answer this time. I knew Kenzie wouldn't. He did!

He finally decided that maybe he should answer in case it was me because they realized they couldn't track me anymore. He tried to describe where he was, but his description wasn't really what I was understanding, so I continued to wander a little back and forth.

Eventually, I figured out what he was trying to describe, and I finally found them. It turns out they were literally within probably 20 feet of me the entire time. Yes, I'm not kidding. There were just so many people around combined with my marathon brain that there was no way I was going to find them on my own. But, oh was it nice to finally see familiar faces. And then, yep I proceeded to cry again.

Chapter Twenty-Four

St. Jude Run 2017

I had been training consistently. It was a slow start as I had a long recovery from the marathon, and I really didn't push myself much. I wasn't injured, I was just sort of burned out. I put in the training runs and put in a lot of miles. But, I had begun slacking on my core work. Core work is essential for me in building speed. I really felt like I was kind of just going through the motions if I'm honest. Usually, St. Jude is the highlight of my running season. It still was, but I wasn't happy with my training at all.

This year's run was going to be different for me though as a few of my friends were joining us as runners. This was extremely exciting for me. Kenzie was even going to run. Stephanie and a couple of other friends (Michelle and Roger) and another local woman were joining our team. Having the opportunity to share this experience with them was making this run uniquely awesome. Michelle's husband was going to drive our RV for us. My niece was going to help as a can shaker. This was going to be such a fantastic experience despite my training. I could not wait for them to be a part of it.

This was the first St. Jude run that I didn't have a "goal" regarding mileage. I knew I wasn't as strong as I had been in years past and just wanted to do the best I could. I had Dopey training ahead so unlike other years when I didn't care if I came out injured, I really couldn't afford an injury as I needed to step right into Dopey training. (I'll get to what this is soon.) I don't think that held me back though. I tried to run legs that I thought I should've been able to. Some I was able to do; some I couldn't finish. The legs I did run were certainly not as comfortable for me as they had been in years past, but I kept pushing ahead.

I again could tell the lack of core work, and the lack of real dedication to the training was taking its toll. But, at the same time, that seemed ok in a way. I was just so excited to be sharing the experience that it looked like this time it wasn't about me and what I was going to accomplish. It was about experiencing it all with these people that were so close to me. That was priceless. Each one of them pushed themselves beyond where they ever thought they could. I was so proud to be running with them. That was one of the greatest privileges I will ever experience. God was taking this running thing He gave me and allowing me to share it with others now at the same time.

All together we raised almost $5000 with the group of "my people." That's another $5000 that the children and families of St. Jude wouldn't have had if I had chosen not to listen to God!

Kenzie had seriously questioned her ability to do the run and therefore, really wasn't too excited going into it. She had started the summer with mono and then had to get her wisdom teeth pulled, so she spent the first half of the summer on the couch. This does not make for ideal training.

146

There is a mandatory meeting for our team a few days before the run. This is to make sure everyone is up to date on pertinent information and the logistics of the day. At this meeting, a few St. Jude patients tell us about their journey with St. Jude and how St. Jude has helped them.

This was what flipped the switch for her. She realized who and what she was going to be running for. These are kids that didn't ask to be sick, they certainly don't deserve to be sick, and St. Jude saved their lives. She realized we run for them. We run because they can't. We raise money to help each one of them get the care they need to live! Not everyone has an opportunity to be a part of something like this. And not everyone can run. But, we can run, and we can run for them! We owed it to them to give them everything we had. This is exactly how I feel every time I run this run. Now Kenzie understood. She was now ready to do this.

The next morning, she got up and went out and ran a 3-mile training run on her own. That was her only training for the run. She hadn't run even a mile since her PE final in May.

We get a list of all the legs on the route. I had shown her the route and talked her through how it went. She went through the list and at that point had decided she wanted to run 10 miles. Wow, I was hoping she would do 6-8 miles. She highlighted her chosen legs on her sheet and had a plan.

It's Race Day (Well Run day in this case)

She was doing great on run day. I decided it was best if I just let her do her thing and didn't run next to her. I question that now, but when we run together, I can't let go of my "mom role." As I've mentioned before, I constantly am asking if she is ok, do we need to slow down, do you need water? I drive her crazy. I chose instead to just let her run, and I knew everyone around her would keep an eye on her for me. This probably was the best idea for her as she got to chat with some of our other runners and get to know them a little. Runners are a very special group of people.

She realized she was easily going to surpass her 10-mile goal and went back to her sheet and added some more with a new goal of 16 miles. On our second to the last stop, we get to stop at Lou's Drive-In. At this point, there is a 3-mile leg, and a half mile leg left. She only needed the half mile to get to her 16 miles. However, now she decided that since she was 17, she should run 17 miles. I walked her through how I thought she should do that. She only needed 1 mile on the 3-mile leg, and I knew that the last part of it was pretty much all downhill and flat. I assumed it would get her at least a mile. I told her to ride in the chase vehicle until she reached a specific point and then hop out and finish running the rest. That was pretty much what she did. She finished the run with 17.4 miles! I could not have been prouder of her. And the best part was she said she absolutely would do it again. That's exactly how we all feel after each year's run.

Since Stephanie was running with us, my brother had come with her for the weekend. He knew that I did this run, but he didn't really understand what it was that we did. He hung out with Greg for the day, and they met us downtown at the Civic Center.

We kind of have a routine now that Greg meets me down there and is there on the sidelines to high-five me on the last leg. He then saves us seats inside for dinner while we line up for the parade. He obviously has the car, so then I have a ride home. Well, until this year Kenzie had been his sidekick for that, but she was obviously with me. David was his new sidekick.

They were watching all the different satellite teams come in because he always gets there in plenty of time so as not to miss us.

David just thought it was our team that did this. He had no idea that there were so many teams involved and the magnitude of what this event entails. He was texting Steph telling her all this and how incredibly amazing this truly was. He had a buddy that was working for him that had a niece that was a St. Jude patient at the time. He texted him and said, "Man, you wouldn't believe what these people are doing up here for St. Jude!" This still brings tears to my eyes.

I really cannot put into words what being a part of this event means. It truly is the most rewarding thing/event I have ever had the opportunity to be a part of. I plan to continue to run in it for as long as I'm able.

Chapter Twenty-Five

The Gathering Church

Some local people that had been from Riverside Church were now starting a church in our area. I came across some information about it one Saturday and saw that they were having a service that night. I absolutely knew that Kenzie and I were supposed to go to it. At that point, I had no intention of attending a new church any time soon, but I knew that for whatever reason God wanted us there that night. This new church is The Gathering Church.

The message that night was about being a spectator versus being a participant. This spoke directly to me in terms of running. I had really been a spectator the last few months. I was enjoying watching the journey of my friends and loved ones and was sort of just going along to cheer them on.

This message was God telling me it was time to get back to it. It was time to get serious again and time to switch back to the participant role. I'll forever be grateful for the opportunity to be the spectator in that season, but I'm also glad that it was short-lived, and that God was ready for me to get back to the deep, diligent work. It was time and of course it again was His perfect timing.

Chapter Twenty-Six

Dopey Training & Michelle

It was time to get serious and back into a steady and extremely challenging training plan. Before the marathon ever came into the picture, I had set my goal on the 2018 Dopey Challenge. It's at Disney World, which I'm sure is evident by its name, and occurs in January.

There is only one marathon at Disney World. The other race weekends all have half marathons. So, if anyone is talking about doing a marathon at Disney World, they are talking about the race weekend in January.

The Dopey Challenge consists of the 5K on Thursday, 10K on Friday, half marathon on Saturday, and the marathon on Sunday. This totals 48.6 miles over four consecutive days. I think it's obvious why it's called the Dopey Challenge. Within the Dopey Challenge, you also complete the Goofy Challenge, which consists of the half marathon and the marathon. We have already established that I'm in it for the bling, and the Dopey Challenge does not disappoint, as you earn six amazing medals! One for each of the four races and then one for each of the two challenges.

To complete these races, I needed to do a lot of training, more than I had ever done before this point. This makes it so obvious why the spectator to participant switch was such a perfect message for me at that point.

I had convinced Steph that once again this was an excellent idea and that she should do it with me. I'm so glad she is willing to go along with my insanely crazy ideas. Michelle had planned to do the 5K and the half marathon. So, we had a nice little group of runners started.

Remember Michelle - my friend that was one of our new runners on the St. Jude Run? She had been a member of our little Facebook group and had taken up running once she quit smoking. She saw my posts about running and decided she would try it and see what she could do.

I convinced Kenzie that she should do the half marathon. I tried for the full, but she wasn't going to be 18 by then, and that's a requirement. It was her senior year, and how many kids can say they have done a half marathon by then? Somehow, she agreed. Then, we got my niece Nicole to agree so they could do it together. Now, we've got a real group!

Somewhere along the way during Michelle's training, she decided that she wanted to see if she could run 13.1 miles. She had done a 7-mile training run and two weeks later decided to go for 13.1. When she completed that and then told us about it, I said, "If you can do that, you can absolutely train for a marathon because it is not normal to jump from 7 miles to 13 in 2 weeks!" So, I convinced her to sign up for the full. Unfortunately, the 10K was sold out as well as the Dopey Challenge, so she was only able to sign up for the three races, but she did upgrade to the Goofy Challenge, so she was going to be able to earn that extra medal.

As I'm writing this, I realize that apparently, I can be persuasive in talking people into running crazy races. But, they really are fun, and when you cross that finish line, I promise you will thank me!

This was another one of God's plans all coming together. Up to this point, almost all my training had been just God and I. Training for this challenge, however, was a lot more mileage and a lot more runs than I had ever even dreamed of. Due to the races being spread over a few consecutive days, you need to not just train for distance, but you also must train for the consecutive runs.

I had only been running three days a week since doing the challenges in 2016, so this was a whole new thing for me to get used to. Michelle had never run this way either, nor had she conquered the distances we needed to cover. She asked if I could try and help her with the long runs, and this is how the buddy system started for me.

We were again following the Jeff Galloway plan from the runDisney site, and since she was basically doing the same races, we just adapted to the Dopey schedule. It really didn't differ that much from the Goofy plan anyway. We planned to do all the longest runs together.

This turned out to be perfect for me. I was swamped at the time with my jobs and was easily distracted by interruptions. By having Michelle with me, I couldn't cut runs shorts. The fact that we agreed to meet at whatever time meant I couldn't talk myself out of runs either. I know for sure I wouldn't have done half the training miles I did if not for her.

When the winter temperatures are low, it can get pretty tough to motivate yourself to get out there. This is also a great reason to have a buddy. Neither of us was going to let the other one off the hook. I should mention, though, that we didn't always have fantastic runs, but thankfully we weren't both having a bad one on the same day. We sort of alternated on that, which made it that much more entertaining.

Normally if I were doing a 20-mile training run, I would run around Wyoming 4 times. There is a nice 5-mile loop you can do around the outer edge of town. That doesn't sound too exciting right? Yeah, it's not. Since I always ran by myself, I felt this was the safest option for me, so that's what I did. I will admit though when I got to the parts close to my house it was tough to keep going and not just cut the run short. Michelle wasn't up for this. The idea of running the same route four times in a row was an absolute deal breaker for her, thankfully. And it still is!

As our long runs were getting longer, we had to be a little more creative in our routes. She lives in Toulon which is 6 miles from Wyoming. There is a trail that connects the two towns and continues either way. I never ran the trail, because I was by myself. However, now that I had a buddy, we decided that was the route we would take. We started adding mileage by adding on the trail. For example, we could make a loop around Wyoming until we got to the trail, then take the trail to Toulon and turn around and come back, and then finish the loop around Wyoming. That was how we accomplished our 17 and 19-milers.

Then, when it came to the 21 and 23-milers, this was a different ball game. We decided we would start in Toulon and run the trail through to Wyoming, pick it up again on the other side of Wyoming, then on to Princeville, through Princeville, and on to Dunlap. The benefit to this was that it was a very slow downhill route. We couldn't very well turn around and come back because that was a gradual incline, and well you know how I feel about that.

So, she graciously had people willing to pick us up at the end and drive us back.

The first time we did this we were unaware of the fact that there was a section of the trail that was closed between Wyoming and Princeville. To add to this dilemma the wind was 18 mph that day. However, it was to our back the entire trip to Dunlap, which was why we thought this was a perfect plan until we hit the "trail closed" portion. Thankfully Michelle is calm during these types of situations. I, on the other hand, was quite panicked. We HAD to get the 21 miles in, and if we turned around and headed back to Wyoming obviously, we could get to the 21 miles. However, that would mean we had to run into 18 mph wind AND uphill the ENTIRE way back. I did NOT like that option.

Michelle suggested we try going through the soybean field a bit and see if we could pick the trail back up soon. She was convinced it couldn't be out for too far. So, that's what we did. We hiked through the bean field (remember this is rural Illinois). When she thought it was safe to try the trail again, we were met with a fence. Clearly her obvious solution was just climb over the fence! Climb a fence? Are you kidding me? I haven't climbed a fence in at least 35 years! She assured me I could do it and that we would be fine.

I agreed to try because somehow that was less terrifying than the uphill, 18 mph wind option. I did make it over the fence with no mishaps. Once we were back on the trail, the path was only wide enough for one person as long as we kept our right arm stretched out in front of us to push the brush back as we ran by. Ok, not so bad, certainly not ideal conditions, but hey this might just work.

We got a little further down the trail and realized the real reason the trail was closed. The bridge had washed out, and the 3 HUGE culverts were all that were left of it. There was a creek below and seemingly no visible way to cross. "Great, now what?" I was in full on panic mode at this point. Michelle of course was still calm. This creek was pretty far down with steep hills on both sides. I could not see how this was going to work. She told me to stay where I was for a second, and she would see if she could scope out a path to cross.

We were confident if we could get to the other side, we would be totally ok. About this time another runner was headed towards us from the other side. Logically it had to be fine from there on because how else would she be able to get to that point.

I let Michelle do some exploring, and sure enough, she found a way to the other side. A small path that led down our side of the hill to a very narrow part of the creek that was easy to hop over. Then, up the steep bank on the other side with the help of the tree branches to pull yourself up with. We made it. We were on the other side. WOW.

Our training run had now become a full-on off-roading adventure. But, we made it! We still laugh about this. What an adventure. I NEVER would've managed that without her. And you know what? We got our 21-miler DONE! Despite the wind, the cold, the hills, the seemingly impossible obstacles in our way, we continued and persevered.

Pretty much just like life. When you think you absolutely aren't going to make it through something, this is precisely when you need your people. Get your people. Let them help you. Reach out to them. Together you can conquer a lot more than you can on your own. This was a real example of this to me. I was learning an all-new lesson about life.

Even though Steph lived too far away to be with us on any of our training runs, she was an essential part of our training. She was the expert. She listened to all our grumblings. She guided us through the unknowns. She encouraged us on all our difficulties.

She reassured us that we could do this and that we absolutely would do it together.

Up to this point, I didn't reach out to anyone in my life for serious things other than Bobbie. I just didn't open up. I figured everyone else has their own stuff to deal with they certainly don't need to deal with whatever my drama of the week may be. And, I had God, so why did I need anyone else? Really and truly He is enough, but He wants us to have people. He tells us we need people. And He was now showing me that it was absolutely ok for me to have and need people. In fact, that was exactly what He wanted for me.

Chapter Twenty-Seven

Monday Night Bible Study

That first night at The Gathering Church, Debbie (my neighbor that was planting seeds in the very beginning about my relationship with God) introduced me to a few of the women at the church. They were also the leaders of the Women's Bible Study on Monday nights at the coffee shop in Wyoming. One of them gave Debbie her copy of the book that they were starting on Monday at Bible Study. Something was drawing me into this. I don't read (it usually just results in me sleeping) and had never been part of a Bible Study. But, at this moment, I knew that I needed to be a part of this. I proceeded to make arrangements with Debbie and her book, so I could read what they were going to talk about on Monday. I obviously couldn't get the book myself by then. But I did purchase my own and had it soon after Monday. I assured them I would be there Monday night. Again, I just knew it was what I was supposed to do. It was what God wanted me to do. I felt an immediate connection with them and was super excited for Monday.

The book was called *Secrets of the Secret Place*. I quickly realized it was about something called a prayer closet. I had never heard of that before, but it's an actual place (a closet for many people) It's a place that you can go to and literally and figuratively shut the door on everything and spend time with God. Maybe you journal in there, meditate, or pray and chat with God. It's a place that all other distractions can't get to you. I also quickly learned that the other women had prayer closets in their homes. I listened and learned.

I was trying desperately to find this place in my home that could be my prayer closet. It was a place where God wanted us to be able to connect with Him and listen, but I was saddened by the fact that there literally was nowhere in my house that this would work. It probably seems obvious to you where my prayer closet was at this point, but I wasn't "getting it." I'm not sure if I had this saddened look on my face or how she knew, but Debbie said precisely what needed to be pointed out to me. Running was my prayer closet. I had nowhere inside my house to shut the door on everything else, but by closing the door on my way outside to run, I was then entering my prayer closet. Yes! This made sense and was an incredible realization.

We continued to read on and learn. As I kept coming on Monday nights, I didn't say a whole lot, but I felt a connection with all these wonderful ladies and knew they were becoming significant in my life. I love our Monday nights. I miss them terribly when I can't be there. I was making more connections, and these were amazing Godly women. I had so much I could learn from them, and I was. I eventually did get brave enough to start talking in the Bible Study, but more importantly, I was learning about God and His word and what it all truly means.

These women have become extremely important to me now. Again, God was showing me that He wanted me to have people.

He knew I was ready to grow some more and to do that I needed to be around Godly women. As I was getting ready to send Kenzie off to college away from home and therefore entering a new season of my life, I know that God specifically taught me this so that when I struggle, I would now have people that I could reach out to that were going to help me through those seemingly impossible moments.

Chapter Twenty-Eight

Dopey Costumes

I talked about costumes earlier for Disney races. But, let me tell you the choices on costumes and theme versus no theme for a Disney race can be maddening. Or in my case, it can be overwhelming because I want it to be the "perfect" choice. I have no idea what that even is so "perfect" is obviously tough to figure out.

In many cases Disney races can be just as much about the costume as the race itself. Many people don't run Disney races for a PR. We run them because we love Disney. We love the extra details of the Disney races like stopping to get pictures taken with the Disney characters. Pictures are really important for most of us during these races as well, so obviously we need to look good while we're doing it. Therefore, having the "perfect" costume becomes a high priority.

We went back and forth amongst all of us (Steph, Michelle, Kenzie, Nicole, and I). Princess themed? Some of us didn't want that. Group theme? Well, what group are you going to be? There are never-ending possibilities with Disney. What's the temperature going to be? That must play into the equation because if it's going to be hot, the costume needs to be relatively cool. If it's going to be cold, the costume needs to allow for layers and last-minute adaptations for warmth.

For those of us that were running multiple races our main requirement was that it had to be running clothes adapted to look like whatever character we were trying to "be." Our other condition was no tutus. Remember, Steph had outlawed them after the Princess race weekend. I had banned them after the Tinker Bell races, and Michelle never allowed them to begin with. I mean a 5K or 10K you can get by with some costume irritations but not a half marathon or marathon. I mean think about it, 26.2 miles is hard enough and then to have to mess around with a costume that is annoying you the entire time? No thank you! I know many can do it, but I am certainly not one of them.

After a lot of back and forth and yes, no, and I don't know, we finally made our decisions. Nicole was going to be Jasmine, and Kenzie chose the Tightrope Walker from the Haunted Mansion ride for their half marathon costumes. We handmade a lot of Kenzie's costume as this is not a common costume character choice outside of a runDisney race. Most of you are probably thinking, "What in the world is she even talking about?" If you have never ridden Haunted Mansion, just do a quick search on your favorite search engine for Haunted Mansion Tightrope Walker, and you will be able to see her. If you have ridden Haunted Mansion, she is in one of the paintings in the round room with "no windows and no doors."

Keep in mind, Stephanie and I had four races to plan costumes for, and Michelle had 3, so we needed to start making some choices quickly so that whatever needed to be purchased or made could be done.

There were 3 of us running the 5K - Stephanie, Michelle, and myself. What do you do for that? Since St. Jude was such an important event for all of us and really where they met, we decided we would all wear our St. Jude shirts from the run. That way we could also represent our St. Jude team and more importantly our support for St. Jude.

Then the 10K. Steph and I were the only ones running that one. She had gotten us matching tank tops that were inspired by the "just keep running" signs at the Tinker Bell Half Marathon. That was an easy solution. Two "costumes" down, 2 to go.

For the half marathon, it was suggested that we be the three fairies from *Sleeping Beauty* since there were 3 of us. Green is Steph's favorite color, Michelle likes blue, and I'm a big fan of pink, so hey why not, it works out perfectly. All we needed was a shirt, some sort of bottom in our respective colors, a hat, and throw some wings on our back and bam, three fairies ready to go. The only issue was that the wings couldn't be annoying to us when we ran. We figured if we strategically tacked them to our shirts they wouldn't flop around and certainly weren't heavy, so we should be good. Stephanie conveniently had a green hat she purchased from our 2017 marathon expo, which was perfect for her. Michelle found a blue hat.

I was on a tight budget again (always) and didn't want to spend a lot on "costumes," so I found a $2 white hat and a can of pink spray paint. Yep, I said spray paint. I painted the hat pink, and we added a lighter shade of pink bow and some jewels to it. It was adorable if I do say so myself. However, I do need to give the credit to Kenzie for the decorating of the hat.

Finally, the marathon, what would the 3 of us choose for this? Again, comfort had to be at the top of the list. *Toy Story* is Stephanie's favorite Disney movie, and her favorite character is Buzz Lightyear. She had wanted to try and dress like him in one of our Disney races at some point but hadn't been able to yet. So, there it was... *Toy Story* was our costume theme for the marathon. Michelle chose Jesse as her character of choice.

Remember that Green Army Guy from the "mountain" in the previous marathon? Well, that was such a pivotal point in that race. So much happened in that stretch of the race. I was ready to give up. I was ready to quit. I didn't have 5 miles of walking left in me. I just wanted to be done. God sent my walking angel at that exact moment to ensure that I didn't quit. Then the Green Army Guy that was supposed to be helping, fun, inspiring, and a piece of Disney magic placed at a tough spot on the course proved to have the opposite effect for me. As I thought about running this marathon again, I needed this part of the course to be completely different than that first experience. I needed to be stronger. It was clear to me that I had to choose the Green Army Guy as my character. This choice was so much more than just a costume. There was so much I was saying to myself and trying to teach myself through this choice.

Kenzie had seen some Green Army Guy costume ideas over the previous couple of years and always wanted to put it together, so that helped in the planning process. I used my spray paint technique on a hat again. Kenzie made me some "weapons" out of felt that I could attach to my water belt. We tried to dye shorts, but the green never came through. That eventually wasn't going to matter because the temperatures were going to be too cold for shorts anyway. I managed to find both a long sleeve and short sleeve green shirt. I even found some green leggings. At the last minute, I remembered we had a green tutu from one of Steph's original costumes during Princess weekend. Yes, this could work. I mean clearly the Green Army Guy doesn't wear a skirt, but it could work for a girl, right? And it was the perfect color that blended with all my other greens. Since I had to wear the leggings due to the cold weather, I had no fear of the chaffing from the tutu like before, which was the reason I had banned them in the first place. Costume complete.

I don't think we could've found any more "perfect" "costumes." *Toy Story* is about toys that play together. They help each other out. They use their imagination. They pick you up when you are down.

One definition of an army is "a large number of people or things, typically formed or organized for a particular purpose." Now, the 3 of us certainly didn't make up "a large number of people," but we were there together to accomplish this marathon. We were there to play together, run together, pick each other up, help each other out, to get through this race start to finish TOGETHER.

In the previous marathon, I had my God-given walking angel that I will be forever grateful for, but this time it was different. God had started teaching me that I needed people. I needed to start letting people in. It was good for me. Having Steph and Michelle through the entire training process. Steph via constant texting and Michelle locally and on training runs was exactly what I needed to complete this monumental race.

Having them run the race with me was perfect. We were an army together. Sure, we could've done it on our own, but not nearly as well. We needed each other. Each of us had strengths and weaknesses that all molded together to make one perfect team. I needed my team, and they needed me.

One of my must-have pictures was me and the real Green Army Guy in the middle of that "mountain." I wanted to be stronger at that point and not afraid of him. He was my inspiration to train harder and work harder and make this try better. It truly was the perfect choice.

Chapter Twenty-Nine

It's RACE DAY X4

The 5K (Thursday)

The wind-chill for this race was somewhere in the mid-20s. Yep, we're in Florida, and we have a wind-chill. Thankfully we had been watching the extended forecast and knew that it was going to be cold for our races. We planned for layers and even had come prepared with throw-away layers. These were clothes we could take off such as extra sweatshirts, jackets, or pants that we tossed to the side of the road when we didn't need them any longer. This is fairly common for colder races and the clothes are generally collected and donated somewhere, so it is a win for all involved.

I wanted to get there early, but in this case, it ended up being too early. Our resort was very close to the start of the race, so our bus ride wasn't nearly as long as I had thought it could be. This resulted, unfortunately, in us standing around freezing for quite a while before we had to head to our corral. We decided we weren't getting there that early for any of the other races, a little extra sleep would be a much better choice. We agreed that meeting for the bus at the resort by 4:00 am was going to be plenty early. Again, lesson learned. Other resorts would require a much earlier bus time. Side note - In my opinion staying on Disney property is a must-do for a race weekend. They offer complimentary transportation for the races from the resorts which relieves a lot of the stress and worry about trying to get yourself where you need to go. Personally, this is a huge thing for me!

We had planned to all stay together for every race. We had also agreed that we were going to take a picture at every mile marker.

Michelle, Steph, and I were finally off and running. It didn't seem quite as cold once we were able to move and run, but it just took so long to be able to get moving. Anyway, we were on our way. We did stay together, and we stopped at the mile markers for pictures. We had a great time together with a lot of laughter! We didn't break any speed records, but that was fine. It was a Disney race, and most people don't do them to get a PR, especially not the 5K.

We loved it! We honestly just had a great time together enjoying those 3 miles around Epcot. Race 1 complete! Off to get a little rest and some park time with the family.

The 10K (Friday)

The adjustment on our meeting time worked perfectly. We had no issues. This one was just Steph and I, because as I mentioned earlier, Michelle was not able to get into the 10K or Dopey because the registrations were sold out.

Steph and I had a great time. We ran a decent/solid run the entire race. We did continue our streak of stopping at every mile marker. We even stopped for a picture with the Genie from *Aladdin*. It was so cold she was even able to sport her favorite Dunkin Donuts stocking hat. Another good race in the books, and we were officially 6.2 miles closer to our 48.6-mile destination.

The Half Marathon (Saturday)

Michelle was back with us again for this one, as well as Kenzie and Nicole. Kenzie and Nicole were going to run together while the other 3 of us were going to stick together. If you remember from before, we decided it wasn't a good idea to have me run with Kenzie because I'm always asking her if she's ok. So, running separate was the best plan. I had, however, given them the whole low-down on the race and what to expect and when. I knew they would be ok and besides, they had each other. They were young and in good enough shape that there was no threat of them getting swept (remember the balloon ladies and the 16 minute per mile pace?) unless something seriously went wrong. And they ALWAYS have fun together no matter where they are or what they are doing!

We had decided we would try and stick with intervals because we knew that with the longer distance, it would be vital for us to be able to still have something left for the marathon the next day.

My hamstring had gotten quite annoyed with me from the miles through the parks during the day and then the races on top of that. There were a few times when my knee was acting like it hated me, but nothing too terrible that I couldn't continue.

This was the first race that took us through Cinderella Castle. I cannot tell you what an incredible site that was. I know I said it before, but as a runner and huge Disney fan, this would land up there in the epic category. We stopped for the picture in front of the castle, of course. We did a group photo, and we each got our solo pic.

We also kept up with our mile marker pictures. It turned out that continuing to hunt for the mile markers distracted us enough that we weren't focused on how much farther we still had to travel. I had my phone telling us our speed and distance. But, my phone gets ahead of the actual distance somehow, and as we continued it got even further ahead. Eventually, the phone was about half a mile ahead of the mile markers. So, we had a half mile to search for it. We then had to decide which side of the course it was on and somehow wiggle our way through the crowd of runners to get to that side without hindering anyone else's run. That should probably be an official challenge within the challenge, to be honest. There were many times that this was the most challenging task. But, after another 13.1, the streak remained alive.

We crossed our half marathon finish line, finally! I had set up the runner tracking so that I could keep track of Nicole and Kenzie and know how they were doing. They weren't too far behind us thankfully. Once we finished, it turned really cold really fast, and we weren't interested in hanging out any longer than we needed to.

They finished, we found them, took a few pictures, and moved quickly to the bus to try and get warm. The girls had completed their first half marathon! I'm so proud of them as this is not something that many people have the opportunity or even want to try to do. And, more importantly, it is NOT easy by any means. However, I'm not sure either of them is in a huge hurry to do another one. But, the point is they both did it and finished!

The Marathon (Sunday)

I need to tell you that by Saturday night, I was done. Steph and I were chatting and waiting on someone, and I just told her I couldn't do it. I was exhausted. The 3:00 am alarm every day, the miles we had already run, the miles we were putting in at the parks, the planning for the races, the planning for the park time... it had all just taken everything out of me. I was done. At that moment I was ready to forgo the medals, and I told her that they could just do it without me. The idea of still having another 26.2 miles ahead of me the next morning seemed utterly impossible. I mean I could barely walk down to the lobby. Thankfully she was able to talk me out of this. This is another great reason we need our people!

We had trained so hard. I had to trust in that. God hadn't brought me all that way to quit and not show up for the final race. Granted it was 26.2 miles, so it's not like showing up for a 5K, but I couldn't come all that way and not finish. I would have forever regretted that choice. It was my idea in the first place to do this crazy Dopey Challenge. There was no way she was going to let me bow out. We ate some ice cream (because ice cream makes everything better) while we had this chat, and she assured me that I could do it, that I would do it, and most importantly we were doing it together.

I did get up that morning, and although I wasn't wholly rested, I did feel better. We had again decided we would do intervals. We were going to try a 1:1, one minute of running followed by one minute of walking. We also decided we had to be much better about sticking to this than we had the day before for the half. We were all over the place with this on that one. But, given we were traveling twice as far and were already exhausted, we needed to stick to the plan to have the best possibility of success.

Within the first few miles, my knee was acting up again. It just got a weird pain, and then it would go away. It did this a few times, but thankfully it went away after that, as I was quite afraid of 26 miles with a knee that was already hurting after 2 miles. However, it was in the back of my head that I needed to be cautious with it.

With our mile marker streak still alive, we continued with that adventure. Again, this worked really well as a distraction. I will admit that the thought of having to go twice as far as we had the day before was quite frightening and overwhelming, but I had my girls/my army/my team, and we weren't going to not do this. We were sticking with it 1 mile at a time.

I had also had some "must do's" for the races besides the mile marker photos. I wanted the castle pictures of course. I wanted some character photos if the lines were short enough. We had taken pictures in front of Spaceship Earth at each of the other races because all four races ended in the same area, so we would again need to do that photo.

If you are in any Facebook groups, there are certain people in those groups that post a lot of great information. Often, they are the admins of the group, but sometimes just members. I find that I learn a lot of great info from these people. There were a couple of individuals that if we saw them on the courses, I needed a picture with them. They are almost like a "celebrity" in a way.

I also wanted to ride Expedition Everest. Yes, you are reading that right. If you aren't familiar with this, Expedition Everest is a roller coaster at Animal Kingdom. It's awesome! You hit the halfway mark of the marathon just before reaching Expedition Everest. If you are in an early corral and have a decent pace, you can plan to try and ride this while you are in the middle of your race. You ride, and then get right back on the course and keep going. The course goes right by the ride, so you aren't even going out of your way. I thought this would be an awesome thing to get to do so it was absolutely on my list.

We also wanted to stop near the finish line and either get a Mickey pretzel or Mickey ice cream and have those with us for our finish line photo. Again, sounds super cool right? Given it was cold, we had decided we would go for the pretzel rather than the ice cream, and honestly after 48 miles the pretzel and salt were going to sound way better than ice cream. I know, I can't even hardly believe I'm typing that as I am a huge fan of ice cream.

My stomach was bothering me off and on so, unfortunately, I was unable to drink much of my fuel, every time I did, my stomach hated me. I could sip water, but the water wasn't going to sustain me for the entire race. We continued on and unfortunately, I had to stop periodically for the bathroom.

We were getting close to the halfway point and Expedition Everest but were a little behind schedule due to my bathroom breaks. Apparently, we were so focused on getting to Expedition Everest that we ran right past the 13-mile marker. Thankfully we didn't get very far before we realized it. We got confirmation from other runners that we had in fact missed it.

Ok, now we must decide, do we go back for the picture or do we skip it? So far, we hadn't missed a mile marker and only had half the marathon to go. Do we break the streak, do we grab someone else's photo later and put ourselves in the pic (with their permission of course), or do we go back? Well, we decided to go back. Ok, the reality is more like I decided we were going back. Steph was not very happy with this decision because I was seriously going to make them go back and cover ground we already ran past. We laugh so hard at this part of the story every time we think about it. She had an extremely valid point and was probably the most logical thinking of the 3 of us at the time, but we still went back. We got a lot of grumbling from other runners. They kept telling us we were going the wrong way, yeah, we knew that, but we couldn't miss the picture.

We got our picture and then moved on. Really it wasn't that far that we had to backtrack, but in a marathon, even 10 feet can feel like forever. We made it to Expedition Everest finally. Unfortunately, the standby line was showing a wait time of 20 minutes. We couldn't wait. I was able to make that call quickly. By the time we waited through the ride cue, then rode the ride, and got back to the course we were going to be looking at almost half an hour or more if nothing went wrong. We had a decent buffer on the balloon ladies, but we couldn't risk a half hour of not moving forward. We still had 13 more miles to go, and if anything were to happen to slow us down, we could potentially run the risk of not finishing. That was not an option, so we just ran right on by it.

Steph was much happier with that decision. Again, she had very valid concerns about riding this ride. Stopping for so long and then riding could cause our bodies to seriously get out of running mode and cause us all sorts of problems we didn't need. Her body is trained much better for these distances than Michelle or I. So, in the end, it was clearly the better choice.

I had a brief negative moment where I was afraid that the reason we didn't get to ride Expedition Everest was that God knew that I would have some knee issues later in the race that would cause me to have to slow way down and that I would need that time buffer. They quickly assured me that that was not the case. But, I knew that it had happened for a reason, and I was about to find out that reason.

When we got to the 14-mile marker, I saw one of those Facebook people that were on my list. I was starstruck I guess you would say. It's hilarious really! They knew about him but hadn't paid enough attention to know what he looked like. I knew it was him though. I asked if I could get a picture with him to which he was happy to agree. He videotapes most of his Disney races and was recording at that point. So, I was even going to be in his video. This was so cool! I mean seriously, he probably started in corral A, which was WAY ahead of us. There were like 25,000 runners doing this race, and we happened to run into him at mile 14. Now I knew why we weren't supposed to ride Expedition Everest. Not only would it have been bad for our running ability at that point, but it was so that we could catch up to this guy. God, once again, had a wonderful and much better plan than mine!

We continued and were back to having a great time. We kept up our antics of mile marker pictures, zigging and zagging trying to figure out where they were, chatting about every bit of nonsense you could think of, appreciating the details in some of the other runner's costumes, and all sorts of crazy things.

We knew that the Wide World of Sports Complex was coming soon. But before that, wonderful strangers were lining the streets. They had boxes of Kleenex. I never would've thought that a Kleenex at that point was going to be super exciting, but oh wow that was awesome and perfect timing. Others had bags of pretzels. I seriously have never tasted pretzels that good. They seriously were just regular pretzels, but at that point in the race, they have a whole other level of yum! Ok, yes, apparently at Disney races you forego every single rule of safety your parents tried to teach you. You take anything and everything from perfect strangers, and you eat it without any question as to whether it's safe or not.

And then the jelly beans, oh man, the jelly beans were terrific too. Again, they were just regular jelly beans, but apparently everything tastes better after about 17 miles. And, yes somehow, I couldn't drink my actual fuel stuff designed to help me in a race without my stomach getting upset, but I could eat these pretzels and jelly beans. I still have no idea how that worked out.

The Wide World of Sports Complex is known as the most horrible, never-ending part of this course. You weave around in there for what seems like forever. It gets a bad rep honestly. This is where you hit mile 20, and nothing is good at mile 20, Disney magic or not, I don't know how anyone can make mile 20 exciting. But, Disney does their best.

I'm not sure how many miles we cover in there, but it seemed like a ton. Anyway, we were winding around the complex, and come to mile marker 18 and guess who we ran into again? Yep, the same guy from mile marker 14! More pictures with him, and this time he recognized us. I mean, I was dressed in the green army guy costume, so it was a little hard to forget especially after only 4 miles. We continued winding around. I was confident we were almost done, but nope, we still had a way to go. We finally made it to mile 20, and then I knew we were close because I knew where mile 21 was and it wasn't in there anymore. We finally made it out and back onto the roads.

We were coming up on that mountain from a year ago. I could see it. This time was very different though. When we reached that point in the race, we were ready to be done, but not ready to quit. There is a HUGE difference between the two. We were having a great time laughing and carrying on. We were complaining the whole time, but none of us were ready to quit. We had come too far, and we truly didn't care how long it took us, we were going to finish. Ok, really, we did care. We didn't want to be out there forever. And, we didn't want to get swept (we weren't in any danger of that at this point). Other than all of that, we didn't care. We just wanted to keep going together!

When we came to the Green Army Guy, he recognized me (because we were twins!) He was happy to see one of his friends, and I was so excited to see him. I had no fear of him this time. We took a few great photos and made some great memories. I did get my photo with just him and I. It will forever be one of my favorite pictures from a race or otherwise.

I had accomplished what I had hoped for. This was a much different mountain for me than the previous year! I had learned. I had grown. I had gotten stronger in so many ways, and I conquered that mountain a totally different person than I was the year before!

We continued and finally made it to Hollywood Studios. We aren't in Hollywood Studios very long, so we got through there and headed the direction of the Boardwalk area.

I'm going step away from the race a little bit here. Up until this point the whole focus had been based around the races, which under the circumstances needed to be the priority. However, it seemed only fair to at least give the guys (my husband Greg, my brother-in-law Denny, my nephew Kyle, and my brother David) something fun of their own to do. So, I set them up with a bass fishing excursion to do while we were running the marathon. None of them had ever fished at Disney, and they all love to fish, so I figured it would be a great thing for them to try. I set it up for 10:00 am - 2:00 pm. This was perfect because we would be done with the race before they were done fishing.

They had a great time with this. They were able to fish in the Epcot Lagoon as well as all around the Boardwalk area! Can you imagine? If you love to fish, how much more exciting would it be to fish at Disney World? And, yes, they caught a lot of fish!

David had been texting Steph a little and told her they were fishing in Crescent Lake near Hollywood Studios and were watching the runners go by. We thought it would be super cool if we could see them.

We could see a few boats out on the water but at first weren't sure which one was them since we were still far away. As we continued to run, they could see us. (David was still texting Steph) Again, apparently, my bright green army guy costume was quite noticeable from everywhere. They happened to be fishing about 10 feet off the shore we were going to run past. We finally made it to where they were and were able to get close enough that we took a selfie from the bank with all of them in the boat behind us. That was super cool and will always be one of my favorite pics from the race.

We continued, and when we came upon the bridge crossing over the lake, guess who was there to greet us? All the girls! My sister-in-law Jennifer, niece Nicole, and my sweet girls Ashley and Kenzie were all there cheering for us! We did not expect to see them. They had been tracking us on one of the apps, and since we were staying at the Dolphin and Boardwalk Resorts for this trip, they were right there. It was super easy for them to find us. Again, what a great surprise and an excellent way to motivate us for the last mile and a half or so of the race.

Most of the time our families can't really be a part of the running process. Unless of course they run too. They aren't with us during the training runs and all the ups and downs that we go through during those. They aren't usually at the races unless they meet us at the finish line or purposely find a spot on the course to come cheer us on. Even though they aren't generally a part of it, they still are a HUGE motivation in being able to conquer these HUGE goals. We know they believe in us. We know that even if we can't see them, they are cheering for us. We know that they will be proud of us when we reach the goals! So, having an opportunity to see your family WHILE you are running a very challenging race is HUGE! I cannot tell you how incredible it was to see their faces! Words truly can't describe it!

We finally made it into Epcot and the World Showcase. We were still doing our 1:1 interval. At this point, we had about a mile or so to go. Ideally, we could've just run the rest to get done faster. Unfortunately, Michelle had a toe that was very angry with her and wasn't allowing her to go much more than a slow run.

And, then there was me! I was worse. Since I couldn't fuel myself due to the stomach issues, I was really dehydrated and feeling quite nauseous. I could handle a slow 1-minute run but needed it only to be 1 minute. As much as I would've liked to, I absolutely couldn't go any faster for fear of vomiting. (Nobody wants to vomit around the World Showcase! That would not be magical.)

We stuck together despite our issues. We did decide that we wouldn't stop for the pretzel. We just wanted to finish, and we figured I probably wouldn't be able to eat anything anyway. We got our final Spaceship Earth photo and headed to find the 26-mile marker. There wasn't a lot of room by it, but we got our photo anyway. And then, there they were - the Gospel Choir. This was also on my list. I wanted a picture with them. We opted not to take the time to try and do a real photo. We just stopped for a selfie. They are so amazing and sound beautiful. It is such a perfect end to a magical course.

We headed off for the final stretch to the finish line. We could finally see it! We crossed, all 3 of us TOGETHER! We did every single step of those miles together, and we had finished! What seemed impossible so many times during training and throughout the trip was now completed! We did it!

We headed to get our medals, and much to our surprise they gave us a Mickey Ear Hat in celebration of the 25th anniversary of the marathon. What was funny was we had seen quite a few runners in the Boardwalk area with these hats on. We knew they were runners because they had their medals proudly displayed around their necks, but we didn't put it together that they had gotten the hats when they finished. We just hadn't put it together where the hats came from and that so many of them had them. Marathon brain at its finest.

I'm glad we didn't figure it out because it remained a complete and wonderful surprise when they gave us ours. Of course, this brought my tears of joy to a whole other level. How super cool that was! We were given our challenge medals and headed off to get our special finish photos taken and then headed to the bus to get back and clean up.

This is one of the most memorable and amazing weekends of my life. I will forever cherish the memories we made on those 48.6 miles. It was a true gift that God so graciously gave to me. The memories we made on the courses were truly priceless. I cannot put into words how special it was and how much more memorable it was having traveled all those miles with Michelle and Steph. I honestly could not have done it without them, and I understood completely why God wanted me not to have to. He had shown me that yes, I could do these things on my own, well really with just Him and I. But, He was now teaching me that He wanted me to have people and that it was ok to let them in and let them help me when I'm struggling as well as to share the amazingly awesome experiences He had planned. He will undoubtedly always be there and in control of the plan for my life, but that having people that I can turn to and count on is vitally important too.

Chapter Thirty

Life is a marathon not a sprint

I've been hearing this quite often over the last year and a half. Maybe I had heard it a lot before, but it just never had any significance to my life, and therefore, I hadn't noticed it. The first time I remember noticing it was during the message at church a couple weeks before my first marathon. Good timing, huh? Nope, God timing!

Until a few months ago, I had been focused on the actual race part of the marathon and the ups and downs, highs and lows, trials and triumphs, that you endure while running the actual marathon because, well 26.2 miles is a long way to go and you will endure a lot of stuff over that time. I can promise you this, that for most of us, it is certainly NOT going to be 26.2 miles of effortless perfection.

A local church had a special event where they were showing some presentations from the IF Conference. Most of the speakers mentioned this phrase about life being a marathon, not a sprint but one kept mentioning the training necessary for a marathon and that

185

you must train your body and your muscles to endure and persevere to be able to go the full distance.

When we broke into our small groups someone in our group mentioned that she wished the speaker had given us real-world examples of how to do this. This building of muscles thing, how exactly are we supposed to do that? What does that look like? I questioned this for a few days and came up with this. When training for a marathon, you do need to run and train. There are of course some people in the world that can just go out and run 26.2 miles and be fine. Most of us, however, need to run and train a lot leading up to the race.

Many follow a training plan that was created by experienced runners that we can trust will work. We run training runs each week of varying lengths gradually increasing the long run distances. We seriously don't run 1 mile one week and jump to a 15-miler the next. It's a slow and steady process.

It's also necessary to focus on fueling and hydration. Without these, your body will not be able to endure the extreme stress you are putting on it. We need rest. This is huge. Your body must have time to rest and recover so it can stay healthy. When it gets closer to race time, we start doubting our plan, doubting our training, doubting our fueling. But in this place, you must step back and remind yourself to trust your training. This is essential.

So how does this translate into being useful in the marathon of life? Training is KEY. Most of the experiences and lessons come from the training, not the actual race. To me, it makes sense that we HAVE to commit to the training. God has given us access to so much in the way of training to learn and grow in Him so that we can finish the marathon of our life that He has designed for us. The question is how do we train? How do we really train? Here are my thoughts.

Training runs = Going to church. Most of us don't go to church more than once a week, but we also aren't trying to complete our "life marathon" over the course of a few months, so it's ok. But, you need to go so you can hear the messages He has for you. He tells us to go. Without the training runs, it's challenging to do the long runs. The shorter training runs keep your body moving. They keep you focused. They help you maintain your muscle memory to be able to endure the longer runs. Without the weekly messages at church, it is difficult to maintain a strong, healthy, and consistent relationship with God.

Long runs = Maybe are conferences, weekend retreats, or something like that that is a TON of great info that you receive over the course of more than just an hour or 2 like a weekly church service. Something you don't go to all the time but is a "wowzer that was amazing and exhausting at the same time." Something totally out of your normal comfort zone but once you have finished is like man, I wish I could experience this feeling every single day. The long run is something most of us are very scared of because it is going to take us somewhere we've never been before, makes us push harder than we've ever pushed before, exhausts us to levels we've never been before. It's a place way beyond our comfort zone of regular shorter training runs, but it is KEY to the process. Maybe this is fasting, a mission trip, a service project. Whatever pushes you way past your comfort zone on your God Journey is your long run.

Stretching/strength training/core work/rest = Prayer. I know there's a lot that I'm lumping together here, but they all seem like prayer to me. Sure, you can train, and many people do without doing these things, but you aren't going to reach your true potential and abilities without putting the time in doing these things. I have learned that if I don't stick with my stretching, I CANNOT run consistently without being injured. I simply can't. My body is not designed like that. I've also learned that one of the keys to me getting a little faster is being extremely dedicated to core work. Sure, I do ok without it but, with it, I do so much better.

Resting is essential, my body needs to heal. It needs to rest and recoup from the stresses I am putting it under. If I don't let it rest adequately, I again risk injury. Prayer is ALL these things to me. Without it, I'm certain to get injured. It doesn't mean of course I'll never experience an "injury," but I know without it I will struggle greatly with "injuries" (struggles of life, stresses, etc.).

Prayer is so important. Praying and declaring EVERYTHING. Good times, bad times, whatever, whenever just keep praying. Most of the time I don't see instantaneous results, but over the long-haul when I look back, I see that without being consistent here there was NO WAY I could've made it through.

Fueling/hydration = His word/music. I've lumped these together because I think most of us are at different places on how we connect with His word. Some people have a fantastic understanding of and ability to read the Bible. Some of us are still at the point that we get the basics of it but don't quite understand every word being said. I'm in this zone, but I love worship music! This is where I get a ton of "fueling." This is all I listen to when I'm running and the only station on the radio I listen to. The lyrics speak deeply to me, and God speaks to me through the lyrics. I've also listened to Christian audio books and now am turning to Podcasts. Now, don't think it's just as simple as tuning into something. I, unfortunately, can't eat and drink just anything and expect to be fueled and hydrated correctly for a run. It's just not that easy.

There are going to be foods and drinks that don't agree with you and make not so pleasant things happen. So, it's going to be key to find the right combination and the right sources that work for YOU. For example (and this is just the simplest of examples) I CANNOT have dairy within 2 hours of running. It will give me cramps. Some podcasts have been the perfect message for me where others have been not so helpful and even negative for me in my season. Anyone that knows me knows that I love cupcakes. Unfortunately, cupcakes are not going to be a good fueling option for a run. I need to focus on protein, good carbs, veggies, and water.

An occasional cupcake isn't going to be horrible, but I can't endure runs by fueling with cupcakes. What is your cupcake? Maybe it's something like social media? (It could look like many things. These are just two examples I'm using) That's not a place for fueling. You can get some great stuff there, but there is also a lot of stuff that will not be good fuel for your "run." If social media is the only place I receive "fuel," I think we can all agree my life is not going to be that great. This is not always easy to figure out but if you pay attention, you can and will find what works and when it works best. This is a learning process and essential to the training plan.

Training partners/buddies = these are your people. We NEED people. We need people that we can go to when we have questions about how to run faster, eat better, why was this run so horrible, why does my ankle hurt after I run? We need experienced runners that have "been there, done that" that will help us in our training process. We need people that will run with us. People that are right next to us doing the long run with us, helping us push through and not give up. Maybe they are new to that distance too, but together you are pushing through and not giving up.

The same thing is true in our journey with God. We need people that are strong in their faith. People that know God's word. That have "been there, done that" in their lives that can help us with our questions on how do I...? We need people that whether they have done it before or not will go hand in hand with us through the battles we face and not let us give up. We need "our people." These are the people in your life that you connect with at church, Bible studies, friends, work, ball games, wherever you find yourself crossing paths with other individuals.

But, just like with fueling and nutrition, there will be people that don't work for you. They aren't truly helping you grow in your training. In fact, maybe they hold you back. Maybe they give you "cramps." This doesn't necessarily mean you cut them out of your life (I love cheese, but I can't eat it before I run) but, you need to just learn how they fit to not give you "cramps." How do they fit that they don't hold you back?

Trusting the plan/process = When you are going through battles, having doubt, and experiencing darkness is similar to when we get close to a big race and start questioning our ability to complete the race. This is when we must have faith. We must trust the plan, trust our training. We must trust God! He has a great plan for each of our lives, and He promises to never leave us or forsake us. No matter how bad things seem, how much darkness we are experiencing, how much doubt and fear are trying to break in we trust HIM. He's got us!

I mentioned "the wall" earlier regarding the marathon. (This happens in training runs as well) This is a very real place. Clearly, it's not a literal wall, but is a dark place that feels impassable. It is a place where it seems easier to give up than to go on. It is a place where you feel like you just don't have anything left to keep going. BUT, you must dig deep. Trust in your training. When your "life marathon" reaches "the wall," you again must dig deep. Trust God! Trust His word. Trust His plan for your life. And, trust your training.

You have put in the training that has built the muscles and endurance needed to carry you through. Your training has taught you to persevere, and this battle is no different. Maybe it's a battle you have never fought before (a distance you have never achieved before), perhaps it's a battle you face on a regular basis (the shorter training runs that often seem harder than a 20-miler). You have trained for this. You have built up endurance beyond measure. You are stronger than you even know. You have God's shield of armor protecting you. You CAN do this! You WILL persevere! When you overcome this battle, and when you complete that impossible distance and are on the other side, the reward/joy will be greater than you ever imagined.

There will continue to be battles and "walls," but none of them are impassable with God! Keep training. There will be many great times and blessings in your marathon as well. Your training was/is vital in that as well. Just keep training, just keep training.

Conclusion

What is it God is asking you to say "yes" to?

I'm reminded that when God asks us to do things for Him, we need to take that step of faith and do it. Whether it's something little that isn't very hard or a giant step that feels like you are jumping off a cliff, we need to listen and have faith. My running journey didn't start with running a marathon. It started literally with 1 block. This book has not been written all in a matter of a few sittings. I was called to write it and felt drawn to try and put 500 words down every day. Many days I faltered in that but then I could turn around and put 5000 words together in 3 days.

I'm slowed down by my other responsibilities and tasks, but mostly by the overwhelmingly scary thought of how I would get this book finished. I've never been a writer. I'm completely unqualified to write a book. Where does it go after I put all the words into my computer? How are the chapters divided? How does it get proofread? How does it get published? And so many other scary questions. I don't currently have the answers to any of those questions, but I am 100% certain that this is what God wants me to do.

I nevertheless took the leap. I have made this book a priority. I've given it to God and know that He's guiding me every step of the way. He has not only guided my words but has also guided the rest of the process as it works in His plan and His timing. Clearly since you are reading this, all of those questions have been answered.

I had no idea where this running journey would lead. I had no idea it would lead me to running at Disney or even running half and full marathons. I had no idea it would lead me to raising over $12,000 for St. Jude. I just took that leap of faith and said, "Yes" to God and I ran 1 block and then 2.

The important thing is that we hear God, we listen to what He is telling us, and that we are willing to say yes to whatever He is asking us to do. When we say yes and obey, we allow Him to do His work in us and the people around us. Sometimes the yes is very scary and seems impossible and maybe it is. But if it is from God, you can be assured that it is the right thing and exactly what you need to do. Do not be afraid! Say yes and take that first step. Do not worry about wavering from time to time. If you do, He will bring you right back to it. I have wavered in this book, but here I am committed again to do God's work and write what He wants written. It was on my daily to do list, but I made it the lowest of priorities on most days. I used to do that with running too. But they both had to get moved to the top of the list. Once they get done, it is much easier to accomplish all the other tasks on the list.

Asking me to run

It is so clear now that when God asked me to run all those years ago, He wasn't really just asking me to run. Running was His tool. He was really asking me to say yes to Him. He was asking me to trust Him. He was asking me to build a relationship with Him. He was asking me to have faith in Him and His word. He was asking me to give my life fully to Him. He was asking me to be willing to hear His voice, to listen to that voice, and obey when He speaks. He was asking me to trust the promises that He has for my life and my family's lives. By being obedient and saying yes to these things, I have changed. I have changed dramatically. Is my life perfect and void of struggles? Absolutely not! He doesn't promise that by following Him that our lives will be without struggles and sometimes seemingly impossible obstacles. He does, however, promise that if we give everything to Him, He will work them ALL for His good and be there to carry us through them. Is He done changing me? Again, I say absolutely not! I still have so much more to learn in this walk with Him, and I cannot wait to see where He guides me next. Hopefully the journey continues to not only change me but give me the opportunity to try and help others as well.

So, I ask you. Has God asked you to say yes to something? How did you answer? If he hasn't asked, ask Him what He wants you to say yes to. Maybe you just didn't hear Him when He asked. Ask Him to ask again and pray that you can hear Him this time. When you say yes, your life may not be filled with running and Disney, but I guarantee you that whatever it is filled with will absolutely be greater than your greatest dream. His dreams are so much bigger than ours, and He absolutely wants to give that to us. Will it be easy? No! In fact, it may seem impossible at times. But, NOTHING is impossible with God, NOTHING!